A History of the Vote in Canada Second edition

Published by the Office of the Chief Electoral Officer of Canada – 2007

For information, please contact:

Public Enquiries Unit
Elections Canada
257 Slater Street
Ottawa, Ontario
K1A 0M6
Tel.: 1-800-INFO-VOTE (1-800-463-6868)
Fax: 1-888-524-1444 (toll-free)
TTY: 1-800-361-8935
www.elections.ca

Library and Archives Canada Cataloguing in Publication

Elections Canada

A history of the vote in Canada

Revised and enlarged edition.
Includes bibliographical references and an index.
Issued also in French under title: L'histoire du vote au Canada.

ISBN 0-662-44087-0
Cat. No. SE3-36/2006E

1. Elections — Canada — History.
2. Voting — Canada — History.
3. Elections — Canada — Provinces — History.
4. Canada. Parliament — Elections — History.
I. Elections Canada.

JL193.H57 2006 324.971 C2006-980228-9

Printed and bound in Canada

EC 91135 (01/07)

Eleanor Milne, Chris Fairbrother and Marcel Joanisse
The Vote **(1979–1980)**
Indiana limestone, 121.9 × 182.8 cm
House of Commons, Ottawa

Sixth in a series of sculptures on the east wall of the House of Commons chamber, *The Vote* is a wheel-shaped high relief with a central "X," the traditional mark made on the ballot when voting. The spokes of the wheel represent Canada's rivers, symbolizing the great distances Canadians once travelled to exercise their franchise. The faces represent the various races and the two sexes in the population, all of whom now have the right to vote.

The cover of this book shows a reproduction of the base stone of the sculpture: four heads with flowing hair whose mouths shape, in song, the syllables of Canada's national anthem, "O-Ca-na-da."

Contents

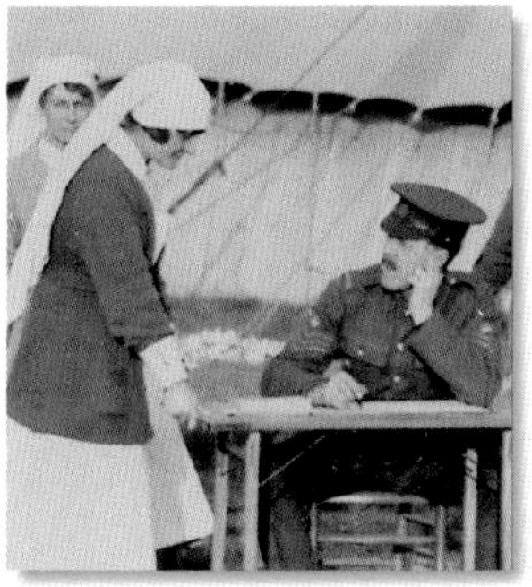

Elections Canada

Preface

WE BEGAN WRITING the first edition of this book in 1995 to mark Elections Canada's 75th anniversary and to offer Canadians a lasting legacy – the fascinating account of the struggles and reforms that shaped Canada's electoral system and led to the guarantee of universal suffrage in the *Canadian Charter of Rights and Freedoms*. First published in 1997, *A History of the Vote in Canada* recounts how Canadians acquired the right to vote over two centuries and how they overcame obstacles to exercising this right. It is the history of an idea and a right, rather than a history of institutions, the latter topic having been extensively explored elsewhere.

The many legislative changes introduced since the book's first publication prompted me to publish this second edition, which includes new sections on challenges arising from the Charter, the reform of political financing, the redistribution of electoral boundaries and Elections Canada's growing role on the international scene.

From a historical perspective, our current democratic rights are a relatively recent phenomenon. For a long time before and after Confederation, fewer people were entitled to vote than were disenfranchised, since the right to vote was conditional upon gender, race, religion, property and other measures of wealth.

The secret ballot – which safeguards the right of all citizens to vote freely and in private, without fear of intimidation – is younger than our country itself, since it was adopted seven years after Confederation.

For more than a century, the qualifications governing the right to vote evolved in a piecemeal fashion. It was not until 1920 that Parliament permanently took control of the federal franchise and created an independent body to administer federal elections. The right to vote was not enshrined in the Constitution until 1982, with the adoption of the *Canadian Charter of Rights and Freedoms*.

The advent of the Charter had a profound impact on the administrative and legislative framework governing the exercise of democratic rights – namely, the right to vote and the right to be a candidate – and of fundamental freedoms, including the freedoms of conscience, of opinion, of expression, of the press and of association.

By constitutionally protecting these rights and freedoms, the Charter recognizes the fundamental equality of each person. Recognition of this equality and of the intrinsic worth of each person, regardless of origin or status, is the founding principle of democracy and the cornerstone of any successful democratic society.

Although the Constitution now guarantees the right to vote, we cannot take the exercise of this right for granted. The various practical mechanisms that enable electors to cast their ballots – such as advance voting, the special ballot, mobile polls and level access at polling stations – are as essential to protecting this right as is the legislation that guarantees it.

Since the beginning of the 1990s, Canada's electoral system has undergone a host of legislative and administrative reforms, some exacted by the Charter – or arising from Charter-based legal challenges – and others linked to Canadians' changing lifestyles and values.

At the same time, Elections Canada has become a modern, professional organization with an expanded field of action. Election management systems have been computerized, the National Register of Electors has come into being, and numerous mechanisms have been put in place to facilitate registration and voting. The Chief Electoral Officer gained a new mandate to establish information and educational programs that give the public a better understanding of the electoral process.

In addition, significant legislative measures have imposed greater controls on political financing, better containing the influence of money on electoral campaigns while ensuring a fair balance between the equality of political players and individual freedom of expression. These measures were further designed to ensure increased financial transparency on the part of all political entities so that electors can make informed and meaningful choices.

This context has increased the demands on Elections Canada. Managing an electoral system that provides electors with more flexible ways of voting, while imposing stricter controls on political entities, has become ever more complex and challenging.

Canada's electoral system is often mentioned as an international model for both its fairness and its effectiveness. Elections Canada regularly provides peer support to countries making a transition to democracy. The agency has also developed successful partnerships with other electoral administrations and international bodies to help maintain its leading edge in knowledge about electoral matters. Canadians can be proud of our international presence, which promotes democratic progress at home and around the world.

In telling the story of a 200-year process based on often very complex laws and regulations, we may have emphasized some viewpoints more than others or overlooked people and events that some may consider crucial to the account. But to quote Leonard Cohen, "There is a crack in everything. That's how the light gets in."* If there are gaps in this narrative, let those "cracks" be an invitation to readers to shed further light on the ideas and events that shaped the evolution of our most important democratic right.

The following persons made the publication of both the first and the second editions of this book possible: Louis Massicotte, political scientist, University of Montréal; Pierre Dufour, historian; Michael Kinnear, historian, University of Manitoba; Lisa Young, political scientist, University of Calgary; and David Jørgensen, freelance writer. I wish to

*"Anthem," *The Future*, Stranger Music Inc. [BMI], 1992.

extend my sincere thanks to these contributors and to all the others, in particular my staff, who collaborated in the realization of *A History of the Vote in Canada*.

Canada's electoral system is continously evolving. And democracy, like life, is ever changing. In a democratic society, each new generation must secure the foundations of the system through vigilance in safeguarding democratic rights and diligence in exercising them fully.

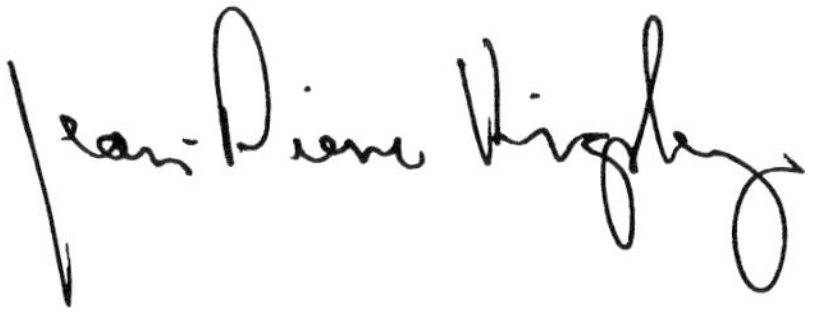

Jean-Pierre Kingsley
Chief Electoral Officer of Canada

Introduction

*"The simple act of voting, of marking an 'X' on a ballot, repeated twelve million times in one day, can overthrow a government without a single shot being fired."**

THE "SIMPLE ACT" of voting – once a privilege conferred on those affluent enough to own land or pay taxes – has become a right of citizenship enjoyed by all but a very few Canadian adults.** Canadians see voting not only as a treasured right but also as a civic obligation – a way of acting on our commitment to democratic principles and protecting our stake in Canada's political life.

The electorate (the body of people eligible to vote at an election) is defined by the constitution and by law – in the case of federal elections, the *Canada Elections Act*. The provisions determining eligibility are referred to collectively as the franchise – the conditions governing the right to vote.

Today, exercising the federal franchise means voting to elect a representative to sit in the House of Commons. Canada's Parliament consists of two chambers: the Senate, whose members are appointed by the Governor General on the advice of the Prime Minister and represent provinces or regions, and the House of Commons, whose members are elected at regular intervals by popular vote. For election purposes, the country is divided into electoral districts – also known as constituencies or ridings – each entitled to one seat in the Commons. The number of constituencies is adjusted every 10 years, following the census, to reflect changes in population numbers and distribution. Since Confederation, the number of constituencies (and seats) has risen from 181 to 308.

Voting follows the first-past-the-post system; in each constituency, the candidate with the most votes is declared elected. After all the constituency results are in, the Governor General invites the leader of the party holding the most seats in the House of Commons to form a government, and the leader becomes the Prime Minister.

Canada's parliamentary institutions have seen considerable evolution and they are, to quote Professor Tom Symons, "the vehicle, the framework, and the practical reality of democracy in Canada." But this book is not concerned mainly with the history of institutions. Many other excellent works offer readers the full story of how Canadians gained representative government and how parliamentary

*Joseph Wearing, ed., *The Ballot and its Message: Voting in Canada* (Toronto: Copp Clark Pitman Ltd., 1991), p. 1. The actual number of votes cast at the general election of January 23, 2006, was more than 14 million – 14,908,703 to be exact.

**Canadian citizens age 18 or over have the right to vote in all but a few limited circumstances. Those excluded from voting in federal elections are the Chief Electoral Officer, the Assistant Chief Electoral Officer and people convicted of fraud or corruption offences under the *Canada Elections Act*.

institutions developed as the federation matured. Instead, this book is about the evolution of the franchise and the body of people who exercise it – the electorate.

The franchise has a long history in Canada. The first elections in New France saw popularly elected representatives, known as *syndics*, chosen by residents of Québec, Montréal and Trois-Rivières to sit as members of the colonial council in the city of Québec. Syndics were not representatives in the way legislators are today. At first, they were intermediaries who simply presented electors' views to council and conveyed council's decisions to the citizenry. After 1648, the council chose two syndics at a public assembly to become regular council members. In 1657, it was decreed that four members of the council were to be elected by the general populace "by a plurality of votes in a free vote" – essentially the single-member plurality system in use today. But throughout this period, the council remained responsible to the king or the governor of New France, not to the people. The office of syndic lapsed in 1674, when Jean-Baptiste Colbert – France's secretary of state responsible for colonial affairs and a critic of representative institutions – reprimanded Governor Frontenac for his innovations.

Parliamentary institutions began to take shape in the second half of the eighteenth century under the British regime; 1758 saw the election of the first assembly with legislative responsibilities, in Nova Scotia, and the other colonies followed suit in the ensuing decades. But these assemblies had limited influence, because executive councils – the real decision-making bodies – reported to governors, not elected councils, and because appointed upper houses could block bills passed by assemblies. Moreover, the franchise at that time was far more limited than it is today. Thus, the capacity of most residents to influence the affairs of a colony was limited. This would not change before responsible government was won in the various colonies between 1848 and 1855. Even then, it was some years before the franchise was expanded to include a much greater portion of the population.

This book is about how the limited franchise of the last two centuries became the universal franchise of today. We examine the evolution of the vote chronologically, focusing on expansion of the right in Canada and on the development of mechanisms to ensure or facilitate the exercise of the right. In advancing the concept of universal male (and later female) suffrage – and the institutional arrangements needed to ensure it – Canadians owe a great deal to ideas made current by British and

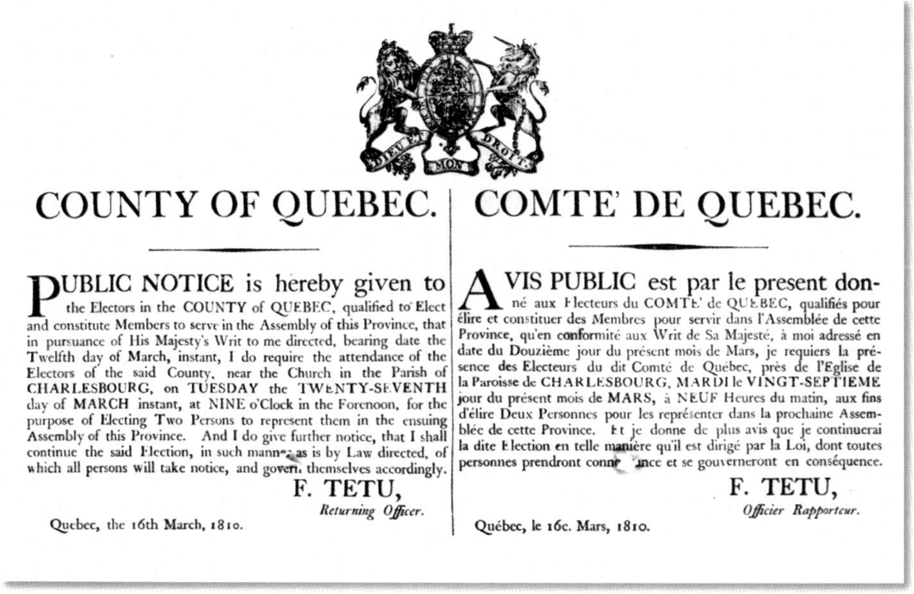

DIEU ET MON DROIT

COUNTY OF QUEBEC.

PUBLIC NOTICE is hereby given to the Electors in the COUNTY of QUEBEC, qualified to Elect and constitute Members to serve in the Assembly of this Province, that in pursuance of His Majesty's Writ to me directed, bearing date the Twelfth day of March, instant, I do require the attendance of the Electors of the said County, near the Church in the Parish of CHARLESBOURG, on TUESDAY the TWENTY-SEVENTH day of MARCH instant, at NINE o'Clock in the Forenoon, for the purpose of Electing Two Persons to represent them in the ensuing Assembly of this Province. And I do give further notice, that I shall continue the said Election, in such manner as is by Law directed, of which all persons will take notice, and govern themselves accordingly.

F. TETU,
Returning Officer.

Quebec, the 16th March, 1810.

COMTE' DE QUEBEC.

AVIS PUBLIC est par le present donné aux Electeurs du COMTE' de QUEBEC, qualifiés pour élire et constituer des Membres pour servir dans l'Assemblée de cette Province, qu'en conformité aux Writ de Sa Majesté, à moi adressé en date du Douzième jour du présent mois de Mars, je requiers la présence des Electeurs du dit Comté de Québec, près de l'Eglise de la Paroisse de CHARLESBOURG, MARDI le VINGT-SEPTIEME jour du présent mois de MARS, à NEUF Heures du matin, aux fins d'élire Deux Personnes pour les représenter dans la prochaine Assemblée de cette Province. Et je donne de plus avis que je continuerai la dite Election en telle manière qu'il est dirigé par la Loi, dont toutes personnes prendront connoissance et se gouverneront en conséquence.

F. TETU,
Officier Rapporteur.

Québec, le 16e. Mars, 1810.

Election Proclamation, 1810

Anyone who met the property and income qualifications (including women) would have been eligible to vote at this election in Lower Canada. Everyone wishing to vote gathered in one place and declared their choice before the assembled crowd of voters (see Chapter 1).

Before the Secret Ballot, 1872
In Montréal, at about the midpoint of the 1872 general election (which dragged on for three months), the Hon. John Young addressed his supporters after the close of a poll. It would be two more years before the secret ballot was introduced in law and six more years before it was used for the first time in a general election (see Chapter 2).

French thinkers and writers of the eighteenth and nineteenth centuries, as well as to the experience of these democracies and of our continental neighbour to the south. While acknowledging this debt, we have chosen to maintain the focus on the path Canada took to give these ideas legislative and institutional expression. At the same time, we must acknowledge other exercises in democracy that took place long before colonization. Prior to the election of the *syndics* and the election of the first assembly with legislative responsibilities in Nova Scotia, Canada's Aboriginal peoples had formed unique social groupings and elaborate systems of government. This book, however, addresses representative democracy since colonization.

This history of the vote in Canada unfolds in four chapters. Chapter 1 examines the vote from the beginnings of responsible government in the colonies that would become Canada until Confederation. In Chapter 2, we look at the period from 1867 to 1919, one of considerable turbulence in electoral matters, including several shifts in control of the federal franchise between federal and provincial governments. Chapter 3 discusses changes in the franchise from the beginning of the modern era in electoral law, in 1920, through to the year 1981. The fourth and final chapter examines more recent reforms in Canada's electoral system in the period following the adoption of the 1982 *Canadian Charter of Rights and Freedoms* – undoubtedly the most significant influence on electoral law in the post-war years.

Focusing on the details of electoral law makes the history of the vote appear extremely complex – an endlessly changing catalogue of rules, regulations and procedures, with many variations in the franchise and its exercise attributable to provincial peculiarities or made necessary by the vast geography and striking diversity of the country. Our goal in this book is not to provide an exhaustive inventory of changes and variations but to sketch the broad outlines of how the franchise has evolved over the past 200 years.

In Canada, as in other democracies, the struggle for universal suffrage was not won overnight. Instead, the vote evolved in piecemeal fashion, expanding and sometimes contracting again as governments came and went and legislatures changed the rules to raise, lower or remove barriers to voting. At first, colonial authorities in England determined who was entitled to vote. Then the elected assemblies of Nova Scotia, New Brunswick and Prince Edward Island gained control of this function between 1784 and 1801.

Among the barriers imposed were restrictions related to wealth (or, more precisely, the lack of it), gender, religion, race and ethnicity. These barriers varied from colony to colony (and voting practices varied from one settlement to another within a colony) and later from province to province (see chapters 1 and 2). Even qualifications to vote in federal elections varied, because under the *British North America Act*, the federal franchise was governed by the electoral statutes in effect in each province joining the federation.

The struggle for universal suffrage was more than a struggle for partisan advantage or political power. As Professor Jean Hamelin points out, resistance to expanding the franchise reflected a general nineteenth-century discomfort with liberal-democratic ideals, an uneasiness with the concept of majority rule and an attitude that equated universal suffrage with social upheaval and disorder created by teeming new urban populations.

As suffragists gradually overcame this resistance, the franchise expanded step by step until the First World War. Then it took an unprecedented leap in 1918: with the enfranchisement of women, the electorate doubled overnight. Since then, voting eligibility has expanded to include many other groups and individuals previously excluded for various reasons.

In 1982, the right to vote was constitutionally entrenched in the *Canadian Charter of Rights and Freedoms*, so that today the only significant remaining restrictions are age and citizenship. Section 3 of the Charter ("Every citizen of Canada has the right to vote in an election of members of the House of Commons or of a legislative assembly ...") cast doubt on the constitutionality of various disqualifications then in effect, giving rise to efforts by those excluded (judges, prisoners, persons with mental disabilities) to petition the courts to have the exclusions set aside. This development gave the courts a significant role in determining who has the right to vote.

Barriers to voting are not only legal or constitutional – they can be procedural or administrative. If citizens have the right to vote but are unable to exercise it because of obstacles inherent in the electoral rules or the way they are implemented, these barriers constitute a restriction of the franchise – one not intended by legislators. The steps taken to overcome such barriers – some of them taken before the advent of the Charter and some of them since – include proxy voting, advance voting, special mail-in ballots, polling-day registration, use of multiple languages in election information, a ballot template for people with visual impairments

Safeguarding Democratic Rights, 1963
During the 1963 general election, the Junior Chamber of Commerce of Kingsville, Ontario, built a likeness of the recently erected Berlin Wall to impress on Canadians the importance of exercising their democratic right to vote. That right was constitutionally entrenched in the *Canadian Charter of Rights and Freedoms* in 1982 (see Chapter 4).

and level access at polling stations, among many others. In short, the Charter not only guaranteed the right to vote but also highlighted the need to ensure that the right can be exercised.

Yet even extending the right to vote to virtually every adult in a society does not guarantee the sanctity of the democratic process. There is an additional requirement that participants in any electoral race compete on a fair and equal footing, and that the voting public be fully informed of the campaign activities of electoral candidates to ensure this equitability. In the last 30 years, sweeping legislation has been introduced to advance these ideals through registration of political parties and other political entities, regulation of political financing and third-party advertising, mandatory reporting of campaign contributions and spending, and other rules central to maintaining due restraint and visibility within the electoral process.

From its origins as a privilege of the propertied class, the vote has become a universal right of Canadian citizenship. As we will see, the road to universal suffrage was not without bumps and detours. Moreover, like its counterparts elsewhere, Canada's democratic system continues to evolve toward the goal of ensuring that all citizens can exercise their right to vote. Each generation faces anew the task of shaping institutions and adjusting processes to serve Canadians and reflect their values and aspirations.

CHAPTER 1

British North America 1758–1866

In the colonies that would later form Canada, the vote was a privilege reserved for a limited segment of the population – mainly affluent men. Eligibility was based on property ownership: to be eligible, an individual had to own property or assets of a specified value or pay a certain amount in taxes or rent.

THE LAW ALSO prohibited some religious, ethnic and other groups from voting. Women were also excluded by and large, though by convention rather than statute. In short, only a fraction of the population could vote. Since then, the situation has improved markedly, and in the following pages we provide a brief history of its evolution.

Evolution of the right to vote was neither consistent nor ordered. The right to vote was not extended gradually and steadily to encompass new categories of citizens; rather, it evolved haphazardly, with the franchise expanding and contracting numerous times and each colony proceeding at a different pace. For example, the degree of wealth needed for eligibility changed several times, with the result that people who had been entitled to vote suddenly found themselves deprived of that right, only to have it returned sometime later. Similarly, laws were adopted from time to time that withdrew the right to vote from groups that had previously enjoyed it.

Moreover, there was often quite a discrepancy between legal provisions and reality. Having the right to vote did not – and does not now – guarantee that an elector could exercise that right. Early in Canada's history, voting conditions set out in the law opened the door to a host of

First Elected Council Meets, 1658
Charles Walter Simpson used gouache, watercolour and oil to depict the Conseil de Québec, established in 1657. Four of its six members – one each from Trois-Rivières and Montréal, two from Québec – were elected by the small number of New France residents who qualified as *habitants* – perhaps 100 of the 2,000 residents. The council had limited powers and did not survive the establishment of royal government in 1663.

Election Security, 1860
With electors casting their votes orally, intimidation and bullying were not uncommon. Dealing with election violence (which claimed at least 20 lives before Confederation) often required the services of the army or police, as in this scene near the Montréal courthouse in February 1860, captured by photographer William Notman.

fraudulent schemes that, in practical terms, restricted the voting rights of a significant portion of the electorate at various times. For example:

- each electoral district usually had only one polling station
- votes were cast orally
- election dates differed from one riding to another
- no polling station remained open if a full hour had passed without a vote being cast

How many voters, living far from their riding's only polling station, relinquished their right to vote rather than travel long distances in often harsh conditions? We will never know. Oral voting made it easier for votes to be bought; it also opened the door to intimidation and blackmail, since bribers could easily tell whether the voters whose votes they had bought voted as instructed. Worse yet, the practice of closing polling stations when an hour had passed without any voters appearing led to numerous acts of violence. To win an election, an unscrupulous candidate could simply hire a gang of bullies to allow his supporters to vote, then bar the way to the polling station for an hour.

Such tactics, coupled with the fact that most candidates supplied unlimited free alcohol to voters during an election, resulted in riots that claimed at least 20 victims before 1867: three in Montréal in 1832; nine in the Province of Canada in 1841; one in Northumberland County, New Brunswick, in 1843; one in Montréal in 1844; three in Belfast, Prince Edward Island, in 1847; two in Québec in 1858; and one in Saint John, New Brunswick, in 1866.

Finally, in addition to voters killed while trying to exercise the right to vote, how many were injured? History does not say, but the following description of a brawl that broke out at a Montréal polling station in 1820 leaves no doubt that voting could often be a risky business:

> Passions ran so high that a terrible fight broke out. Punches and every other offensive and defensive tactic were employed. In the blink of an eye table legs were turned into swords and the rest into shields. The combatants unceremoniously went for each other's nose, hair and other handy parts, pulling at them mercilessly … The faces of many and the bodies of nearly all attested to the doggedness of the fighting.
>
> *Hamelin and Hamelin, 47–48, translation*

Rather than expose themselves to such dangers, some voters, at least occasionally, no doubt relinquished the right to vote. As Canadian electoral law was amended to limit fraudulent practices and outbursts of violence, therefore, it ensured that a growing proportion of the population could exercise the right to vote.

Legislative Assemblies and Responsible Government

Canadian parliamentary institutions began to take shape in the latter half of the eighteenth century. Though this book discusses elections following European colonization, we cannot ignore the fact that Canada's Aboriginal peoples had developed their own systems of government long before the creation of parliamentary institutions in Canada. A well-known example is the Six Nations Confederacy, sometimes referred to as the oldest living participatory democracy on earth.* (Fenton, 68–73)

The first legislative assembly was elected in Nova Scotia in 1758; Prince Edward Island followed suit in 1773, New Brunswick in 1785, then Lower Canada (Quebec) and Upper Canada (Ontario) in 1792. Executive authority still eluded these assemblies, however, remaining in the hands of executive council members appointed by colonial governors, who were in no way accountable to elected members or to the electorate. The consent of an assembly was required for a bill to become law, but bills originating in the assembly could be vetoed by Crown-appointed legislative councillors, and assemblies had no control over executive councillors.

In the first half of the nineteenth century, then, recognition of the principle of responsible government – not extension of the franchise –

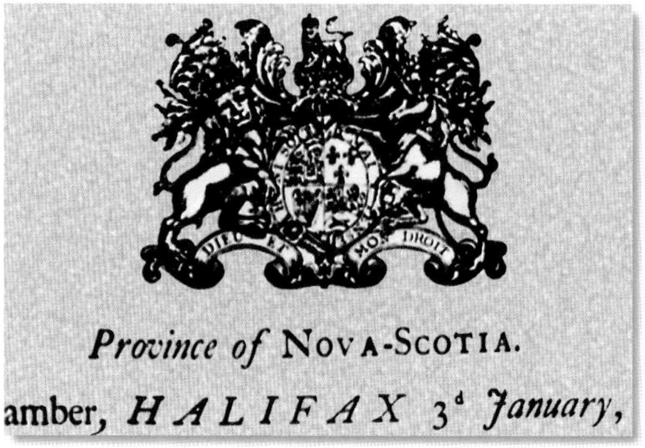
Province of NOVA-SCOTIA.
amber, *HALIFAX* 3d *January*,

Struggle for Elected Assembly, 1757
When Nova Scotia Governor Charles Lawrence ignored his appointed assembly's advice (contained in resolutions reproduced *left*), four of its members published a pamphlet, which they sent to colonial authorities along with a letter of protest. London ordered Lawrence to hold an election, and the first elected assembly in what is now Canada met in Halifax on October 2, 1758.

sparked reform efforts in the colonies of British North America. Politicians known as Reformers endeavoured, first and foremost, to achieve responsible government, with ministers chosen by the majority in the house of assembly (and forced to resign if they lost the confidence of that majority) and accountable to it.

In 1836, Joseph Howe, known as the voice of Nova Scotia, expressed succinctly the objective of the Reformers of his time: "[A]ll we ask for is what exists at home – a system of responsibility to the people." (*DCB* X, 364) In other words, Reformers demanded that governors not be able to do in the colonies what the king himself could not do in England: choose ministers.

Colonial governors' opposition to such a change was backed up in London by successive secretaries of state for the colonies, whose attitude was summed up in a remark by Lord Bathurst, who apparently told a new governor on the eve of his departure for North America, "Joy be with you, and let us hear as little of you as possible." (*DCB* VIII, xxiv) This directive seems to have been followed scrupulously,

*Many scholars date the beginning of the Six Nations Confederacy at the mid-fifteenth century, although a small number argue that the Confederacy began much earlier, even a millenium before the arrival of Columbus.

for until 1828, the colonial office had only a vague idea of the discontent brewing for years in some colonies, particularly Upper and Lower Canada, where rebellions broke out less than 10 years later.

London's response – the 1838 appointment of Lord Durham as governor general, with a mandate to investigate the causes of unrest – did not produce immediate change. Durham recognized that the main source of problems for colonial governments lay in the fact that their executive councils were not responsible to the legislatures. He therefore recommended responsible government for each colony.

Fearing the loss of its authority, the British government rejected Durham's recommendations, apparently on the ground that colonial governors would essentially become independent sovereigns if they began to act on the advice of a council of ministers.

London's inaction soon led to legislative impasse, as Reformers gradually gained control of colonial assemblies and refused to ratify legislation proposed by governors and their councils. The impasse was eventually resolved after Sir George Grey was appointed secretary of state for the colonies in 1846 and promised to grant responsible government to the largest North American colonies at the first opportunity.

The following year, Reformers won the Nova Scotia election; in February 1848 they took office, inaugurating the first responsible government in a British colony. Joseph Howe remarked that this victory had been won without "a blow being struck or a pane of glass broken," (*DCB* X, 365) forgetting the role of rebellions in Upper and Lower Canada a decade earlier. A month later, in March 1848, it was the turn of Reformers in the Province of Canada to bring in their responsible government. Prince Edward Island and New Brunswick did likewise in April 1851 and October 1854 respectively.

Among the chief architects of this fundamental change in the shape of Canadian parliamentary institutions were the following Reformers: Joseph Howe and James Boyle Uniacke of Nova Scotia; Charles Fisher and Lemuel Allan Wilmot of New Brunswick; George Coles of Prince Edward Island; Louis-Hippolyte La Fontaine, Augustin-Norbert Morin and Louis-Joseph Papineau of Lower Canada; and William Warren Baldwin and his son Robert, Sir Francis Hincks and William Lyon Mackenzie of Upper Canada. Thanks to them and other Reformers, Canadians acquired the right not only to elect assembly members but to choose their governments.

The England of George III

While allowing its colonies to have legislative assemblies, London was also deciding, through governors and their councillors, who would have the right to vote. The legislative assemblies of the Maritime colonies gained partial control in this area between 1784 and 1801, while Upper and Lower Canada did not do so until after their union in 1840. It was 1847, however, before London gave colonial assemblies the right to set their own rules on naturalization of immigrants, thereby giving them full authority to determine who had the right to vote. Thereafter, each colony had the authority to confer the status of British subject, but this status was valid only on its own territory; granted by London, such status was valid throughout the empire.

Initially, the rules governing the right to vote in the colonies of British North America tended to be modelled on those of the mother country. In the England of George III – the second half of the eighteenth century – several categories of individuals were denied the right to vote. First, the right to vote was based on property ownership: to be eligible to vote, an individual had to own a freehold (land free of all duties and rents), and this freehold had to generate a minimum annual revenue of 40 shillings, or £2 sterling; this immediately excluded a large segment of the population.

Of the other groups denied the vote, women undoubtedly represented the greatest number. There was no decree or law prohibiting them from voting; rather, they had not voted for centuries by virtue of a tacit convention of English common law. They did not acquire the right to vote in Canada until 1918. (Some women associated with the war effort gained the vote in 1917. For a full discussion of women and the vote, see Chapter 2.)

Nor could Catholics and Jacobites vote. Mostly Scottish and Irish Catholics, the Jacobites were supporters of James II, who had tried in vain to restore Catholicism in England in the late seventeenth century. Shortly after, in 1701, in an attempt to strengthen Protestantism, the English authorities devised three oaths of state designed to exclude Catholics and Jacobites from public office. The first oath was one of allegiance to the king of England; the second, known as the oath of supremacy, denounced Catholicism and papal authority; and the last, the oath of renunciation, repudiated all rights of James II and his descendants to the English throne. Not only was swearing these oaths necessary to hold public office, but electors could be required to swear them before voting.

What is more, the law forbade Catholics to practise their religion, to acquire property through purchase or inheritance, to sit in Parliament and to vote. The prohibition on owning property was removed in 1778, and a 1791 law allowed open practice of their religion again, but they would not be given the right to vote until 1829. Jews also experienced exclusion, though indirectly. They were not explicitly denied the vote, but they refused to take the oaths of state, because they were to be taken "in the name of the Christian faith."

Immigrants and other new arrivals who were not British subjects and had not been in the colonies long enough to become naturalized citizens were the other sizable group unable to vote. Once again, no law or decree prohibited them from voting; rather, common law prevented them from doing

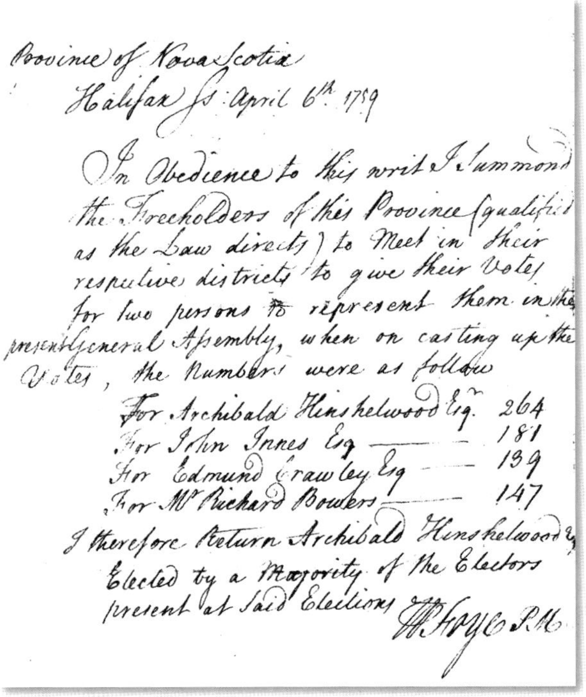
Province of Nova Scotia
Halifax ss: April 6th 1759

In Obedience to this writ I summoned the Freeholders of this Province (qualified as the Law directs) to Meet in their respective districts to give their Votes for two persons to represent them in the present General Assembly, when on casting up the Votes, the Numbers were as follow

For Archibald Hinshelwood Esq. — 264
For John Innes Esq — 181
For Edmund Crawley Esq — 139
For Mr Richard Bowers — 147

I therefore Return Archibald Hinshelwood Esq Elected by a Majority of the Electors present at said Elections

W. Foye P.M.

First By-election, 1759

Governor Lawrence of Nova Scotia issued a writ, dated January 10, 1759, commanding a by-election. The seats of two members, John Anderson and Benjamin Gerrish, had been declared vacant. The colony, which included present-day New Brunswick and Prince Edward Island, consisted of a single constituency. Men over 21 who owned freehold land were eligible to vote. Here, the chief election official at Halifax reports the results to the governor, writing them on the back of the original writ.

PROCLAMATION!

DIVISION ELECTORALE DE MONTARVILLE. — ELECTORAL DIVISION OF MONTARVILLE.

SAVOIR:

Avis Public est par le present donne aux ELECTEURS de la Division Electorale de Montarville, qu'en obeissance au writ de Sa Majeste à moi adresse, en date du vingt-neuvieme jour du mois d'Avril, mil huit cent soixante-et-un. Je requiers la presence des dits Electeurs a la porte de l'Eglise de la paroisse de Longueuil, dans le comte de Chambly, en la dite Division de Montarville,

LUNDI, le troisieme jour du mois de JUIN

prochain a ONZE Heures de l'avant-midi, aux fins d'élire une personne pour les représenter dans le Conseil Legislatif de cette Province; et qu'en cas de demande et d'octroi d'un poll en la maniere voulue par la loi, tel poll sera ouvert le DOUZIEME JOUR du dit Mois de JUIN, a NEUF heures de l'avant-midi, dans la Salle Publique ou a la porte de l'eglise de chacune des Paroisses ci-apres mentionnees, savoir:

Dans le comté de Chambly, les Paroisses de Longueuil, Boucherville, Chambly, St. Bruno.

Dans le comté de Verchères, les paroisses de Varennes, Belœil, St. Antoine, St. Marc, Verchères, Contrecœur, Ste. Julie.

Dans le comté de Laprairie, les paroisses de St. Isidore, St. Philippe, St. Constant, St. Jacques le Mineur, et Laprairie.

Et du contenu de la présente Proclamation, toute personne est requise de prendre connaissance, et de se gouverner en conséquence.

Donné sous mon seing, à Laprairie, ce septième jour du mois de Mai de l'année mil huit cent soixante-et-un.

Officier-Rapporteur.

TO WIT

Public Notice is hereby given to the ELECTORS of the Electoral Division of Montarville, that in obedience to Her Majesty's writ to me directed, and bearing date the twenty ninth day of the month of April, one thousand eight hundred and sixty one, I require the presence of the said Electors at the Church door of the Parish of Longueuil, in the County of Chambly, in said Electoral Division, on

Monday, the Third Day of the Month of June

next, at ELEVEN o'clock in the forenoon, for the purpose of electing a person to represent them in the Legislative Council of this Province; and that in case a Poll be demanded and allowed in the manner by law prescribed, such Poll will be opened on the *TWELFTH* day of the said month of *JUNE*, at NINE o'clock in the afternoon, in the Public Hall or at the Church door of each of the Parishes hereinafter mentioned, namely:

In the county of Chambly, the parishes of Longueuil, Boucherville, Chambly, St. Bruno; in the county of Verchères, the parishes of Varennes, Beloeil, St. Antoine, St. Marc, Verchères, Contrecoeur, Ste. Julie; and in the county of Laprairie, the parishes of St. Isidore, St. Philippe, St. Jacques le Mineur ~~and~~ Laprairie.

Of all which every person is hereby required to take notice and to govern himself accordingly.

Given under my hand, at Laprairie, this seventh day of the month of MAY, in the year one thousand eight hundred and sixty one.

Returning-Officer

Candidate Wins Seat, Then Loses It

Forced to flee his Polish homeland after opposing Russian rule in the 1831 rebellion, Alexandre-Édouard Kierzkowski (1816–1870) reached Canada in 1842, becoming a naturalized British subject in 1847. Kierzkowski, *right*, was elected to the Province of Canada's legislative council on September 15, 1858, but opponents claimed that his property value was insufficient to qualify him for office. After a three-year investigation, a legislative committee declared the election void (not unusual in tumultuous nineteenth-century politics). His challenger at the ensuing by-election (proclamation, *above*) was Louis Lacoste (1798–1878), a political activist in Lower Canada. Lacoste defeated Kierzkowski, 2,042 votes to 2,013.

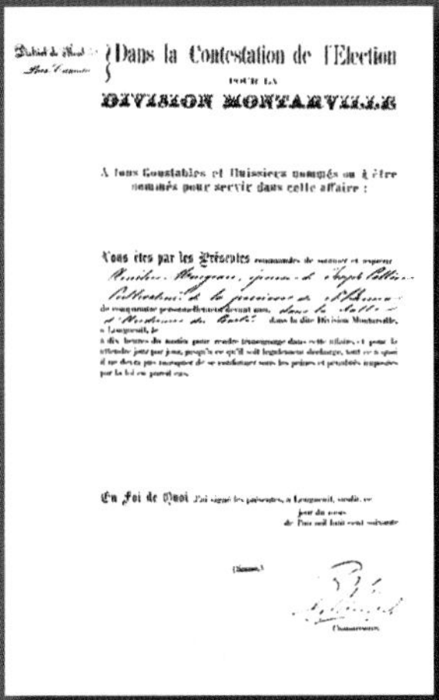

Dans la Contestation de l'Election

POUR LA

DIVISION MONTARVILLE

A tous Constables et Huissiers nommés ou à être nommés pour servir dans cette affaire :

Vous êtes par les Présentes

En Foi de Quoi

so and from owning property directly or through a lease or farm tenancy. In 1844, a law was passed, allowing them to hold property through a lease or farm tenancy, and in 1870, a second law allowed them to purchase landed property directly; but both laws also stipulated that they did not have the right to vote, even if they met the legal qualifications. Since 1740, however, immigrants had been able to become British subjects and thereby gain the right to vote if they met three conditions: they had lived in England for seven years, they had taken the three oaths of state and they had received communion according to the rite of a reformed church (which was, in practice, the Church of England). These conditions prevented Catholic immigrants, as well as immigrants belonging to certain Protestant sects, such as Baptists and Methodists, from becoming British subjects.

On the whole, these restrictions were applied only partially and erratically in the North American colonies because of the different socio-economic conditions prevailing there. The criteria also varied from colony to colony, with the result that those that formed Canada initially – Nova Scotia, Prince Edward Island, New Brunswick, Quebec, Ontario and British Columbia – joined Confederation with appreciably different electoral laws. The nature and evolution of these laws are the main focus of this chapter.

Nova Scotia: Cradle of Canadian Parliamentary Government

In 1713, under the Treaty of Utrecht, France ceded Nova Scotia to England but kept Île Royale (Cape Breton Island) and Île Saint-Jean (Prince Edward Island). The following year, a small British garrison was established at Port-Royal, Nova Scotia, now renamed Annapolis Royal. The 2,000 Catholic, French-speaking Acadians living in the colony at the time agreed to swear an oath of allegiance containing a clause exempting them from bearing arms in the event of conflict with France. In the decades to come, despite every effort to attract them, very few colonists from New England settled in Nova Scotia, while the number of Acadians multiplied at a rapid rate. In the circumstances, the English authorities considered it imprudent to let the colony have a legislative assembly.

Following the War of the Austrian Succession (1744–1748), London finally decided to try to change the population makeup in Nova Scotia by encouraging emigration by non-English Protestants from Europe, mainly victims of religious wars there. Recruited mostly from Germany, but also from the Netherlands and Switzerland, about 2,600 such immigrants accompanied Colonel Edward Cornwallis, governor of Nova Scotia and founder of Halifax, when he sailed to Nova Scotia in 1749. That same year, Governor Cornwallis was given full authority to establish an elected assembly when he deemed it appropriate, but he delayed doing so

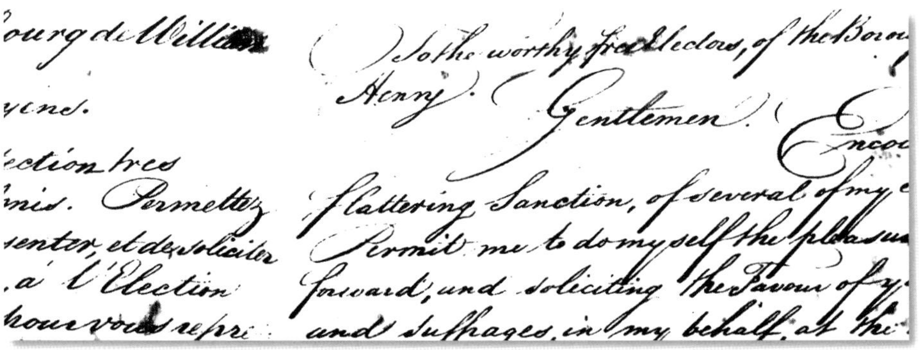

First Jewish Candidate, 1796
Moses Hart issued this announcement, asking for voters' support, but later withdrew his candidacy. Hart's younger brother, Ezekiel, elected in 1807, was prevented from taking his seat by the oath of office, which included the phrase "upon the true faith of a Christian." Jews were also excluded from voting by the oath designed to bar Catholics. Ezekiel's son Aaron was instrumental in having the oath changed in the 1830s.

indefinitely, as the colony was home to three to four times as many Acadians as Protestants.

In 1754, war broke out again between England and France. This time, the British demanded that the Acadians, who had previously remained neutral, take up arms. They refused. The British reaction was to deport them. In 1755, as their homes were burned down, about 7,000 Acadians were herded onto ships and dispersed among the Thirteen Colonies of New England and the West Indies; between 2,000 and 3,000 more met the same fate in the years that followed.

That same year, colonists from New England, particularly Massachusetts, began to settle on the land confiscated from the Acadians, while other immigrants arrived from the British Isles. Thus, on the eve of the American Revolution, Nova Scotia had about 20,000 inhabitants, nearly half of whom had come from New England, the rest being Acadians who had returned from exile or escaped deportation, or Irish, Scottish and English settlers.

The American Revolution changed the composition of Nova Scotia's population considerably. Following the Treaty of Versailles (1783), which recognized the United States, Loyalists – people living in the United States who had remained loyal to the English Crown – fled north by the tens of thousands. An estimated 35,000 settled in Nova Scotia, more than doubling its population. This massive influx led to socio-political tensions that would last for years, but it also prompted the establishment of new Maritime colonies in 1784: New Brunswick and Cape Breton.

When the governor of Nova Scotia called the 1758 election, which would lead to the formation of the first legislative assembly in Canadian history, the population was still quite small and made up of fairly recent arrivals. The conditions for eligibility to vote, therefore, had to be more liberal than in England to yield a sufficient number of voters. With the support of his councillors, the governor declared that any Protestant age 21 or older who owned a freehold of any value could vote. In addition, however, prospective voters could be asked to swear the three oaths of state; this ensured that no Catholics would try to vote and disqualified Jews at the same time. As for women, their status was the same as that of English women. In 1759, however, the governor and his council decided to

Nova Scotia

1758 First elected assembly. Eligible to vote: Protestants age 21 or older who own a freehold of any value.

1783 Assembly gains statutory control of representation and the franchise.

1789 Assembly removes religious restrictions on eligibility to vote.

1848 First responsible government in British North America inaugurated.

1851 Right to vote separated from land ownership, extending the franchise to men over 21 who have paid taxes in the year preceding an election; number of electors increases by 30 percent.

1854 Universal male suffrage adopted (though it does not include Aboriginal people or people receiving financial assistance from government); number of electors increases by 50 percent. Nova Scotia is first colony in North America to adopt male suffrage and the only one to do so before Confederation.

1863 Restrictive rules reintroduced – property ownership again a criterion for eligibility.

1867 Rules in place at Confederation: to vote in a federal election held in Nova Scotia, electors have to be male, age 21 or older, and own property of a specified value.

Partie Orientale de la Nouvelle France ou du Canada
Par Mr. Bellin Ingenieur du Roy et de la Marine Pour servir à l'Intelligence des affaires et de l'Etat present en Amerique communiqueé au Public par les Heritiers de Homan en l'an 1755.
Echelles
Lieues Communes de France de 25 au Degré
Lieues Marines de France et d'Angleterre de 20 au Degré
Nitchik Irinioüetchs ou Nation de la Loutre
Partie de Labrador dont l'Interieur est entierement Inconnu
Pays des Esquimaux
Pays des Attik Irinioüetchs ou Gens du Caribou
Golphe de St. Laurent
Isle de Terre-Neuve
L'Interieur de l'Isle et le Cours des Rivieres ne sont pas connus
Fleuve de St. Laurent
Isle d'Anticosti
Banc a Vert 30 Brasses
Les Bancs de l'Acadie ou l'on fait la Peche
Fond de la Bie. de Hudson
Pie-Koua
Atticameouecs
Cap Cod
Havre de Baston
Cap de Sable
I. de Sable
Belle Isle
Cap de Raze
Les Sept Isles
I. de la Madelaine
Partie du Banc de Terre neuve

New France, 1755 *(left)*
The eastern part of New France, mapped in 1755 by Jacques-Nicolas Bellin, map-maker and engineer to the King in the employ of the French navy. The map is an etching on paper, embellished with ink and watercolour.

Universal Male Suffrage: Nova Scotia, 1854 *(below)*
If they were over 21 and had lived in the colony at least five years, these Yarmouth merchants (photographed by Wellington Chase in the spring of 1855) were eligible to vote under the 1854 electoral law. Property ownership entitled recent immigrants to vote as well. "Universal" male suffrage did not include "Indians," however, and it lasted only until 1863, when property ownership again became a requirement.

restrict the vote to freeholders owning property generating an annual revenue of 40 shillings, as in England.

The arrival of the Loyalists prompted a change in conditions of eligibility. In 1789, the legislative assembly rewrote the rules of the game. Freeholders still had to meet the criteria established in 1759, but the right to vote was extended to anyone who owned a dwelling with his land, regardless of its value; to anyone who owned at least 100 acres of land, whether farmed or not; and to anyone who occupied Crown land by virtue of an occupancy permit. Finally, the legislative assembly abolished religious discrimination in the eligibility criteria, enabling Catholics and Jews to vote. These new measures favoured urban landowners, fishermen and Loyalists, a good many of whom had only an occupancy permit.

Compared to the rules prevailing in the England of George III, those established by the Nova Scotia assembly were quite liberal – perhaps even a little too liberal. In 1797, the assembly reconsidered and tightened the rules once again. In future, those occupying Crown land by virtue of an occupancy permit would no longer have the vote, nor would freeholders who had not formally registered their property at least six months before an election; owners of 100 acres of land or more would no longer have the vote unless they were farming at least five acres of it.

It was not until 1839 that the assembly changed the rules again. It upheld the right to vote of freeholders owning property generating an annual revenue of 40 shillings but withdrew it from owners of 100 acres of land and those who owned a dwelling with their land. However, property owners who met the same conditions as freeholders could now vote. In addition, mortgagors and co-owners were now eligible to vote, as were tenants, if they owned an interest in real property that earned them at least 40 shillings annually.

Twelve years later, in 1851, Nova Scotia took the significant step of detaching the right to vote from land ownership. The assembly declared that anyone age 21 or older who had paid taxes (in any amount) in the year preceding an election could vote. In ridings where taxes were not yet collected, only freeholders with property yielding 40 shillings a year could vote. The same law stipulated, however, that no woman could vote even if she met the legal requirements regarding taxes or property. The assembly added this clause because, during an election held in 1840, a candidate in Annapolis County had tried to get some 30 women who had the necessary qualifications to vote, common law notwithstanding.

In 1854, Nova Scotia became the first colony in British North America to adopt universal male suffrage – and it would be the only one to do so before Confederation. That year, the assembly adopted a law to the effect that British subjects age 21 or older who had lived in the colony at least five years could vote. It kept the rule allowing freeholders with property generating a minimum annual revenue of 40 shillings to vote; this enabled a number of immigrants of British origin to vote even though they had not lived in the colony for five years. Like the electoral law of 1851, the 1854 act contained a restrictive clause stating that "Indians"* and people receiving financial assistance from the government could not vote.

Further change, more conservative this time, came a decade later: the elimination of universal suffrage and a return to more restrictive rules. In 1863, Nova Scotia limited the right to vote to British subjects at least 21 years old who owned property assessed at $150 or more, or personal and real property assessed at $300 or more. The number of eligible British subjects was expected to increase, however, at least in theory, as immigrants now had to live in the colony for only a year to be declared British subjects.

Such were the rules that defined the Nova Scotia electorate in August and September of 1867, when the first Canadian federal election was held.

Prince Edward Island: A "Landless" Colony

In 1758, the British succeeded in taking possession of Île Saint-Jean, where it followed the same policy as had been pursued in Nova Scotia a few years earlier. Some 4,000 French and Acadian colonists were deported, but several hundred evaded capture by seeking refuge in the far corners of the island. In 1763, after the Treaty of Paris, the island was joined with Nova Scotia. Four years later, it was subdivided into 67 townships of about 20,000 acres each; these were distributed to individuals who had earned the gratitude of the British government for services rendered during the Seven Years' War. The lands were granted on certain conditions, one being that they be used for Protestant settlers, who were not to come from other British colonies. At the turn of the nineteenth century, some of these lands were joined, so that a few wealthy individuals, most living off the island, came to own vast expanses of land that they often refused to sell, preferring long-term leases to tenant farmers. By the middle of the century, not even a third of the farmers were freeholders, and it was not until 1895 that the government bought back the last estate from the remaining large landowner.

In 1769, the island was separated from Nova Scotia to form a distinct colony, and its first governor was instructed to establish an elected assembly when he deemed it appropriate. The population, almost exclusively Acadian, was still very small; the governor delayed. Between 1770 and 1773, about 800 Scottish settlers came to the island, increasing the population to more than 1,200, and it was at this point that the governor decided to exercise his prerogative. He restricted the vote to freeholders and planters, but there were practically none of these on the island; almost all the residents were tenants or squatters living on land belonging to absentee landlords. With the consent of his councillors, the governor gave the vote to all Protestants living on the island, imposing no further restrictions related to age, nationality or gender. It was understood, however, that the island would follow the prevailing electoral practice in England, where neither children nor women could vote. For the time being, however, only Catholics were explicitly denied the vote, although Jews were effectively excluded as well, as voters could be required to swear the three oaths.

After the American Revolution, only a few hundred Loyalists joined the Acadians and colonists

*The Aboriginal peoples known today as First Nations were referred to then as "Indians" in both federal and provincial law. We use that term here only for historical accuracy and to avoid confusion in discussing the legal provisions governing the franchise.

The viva voce *system was more in accordance with the institution of the empire to which we belonged and more congenial to the manly spirit of the British people; and he would not therefore consent to abandon it in favour of the underhand and sneaking system of a vote by ballot.*

– C. A. Hagerman, Solicitor General
Kingston Chronicle
February 12, 1831

of British origin. However, a change that affected the electorate was made in 1787. Protestant residents of rural areas would continue to have the vote, but in Princetown, Georgetown and Charlottetown, only freeholders would be allowed to vote; this obviously excluded tenants.

In 1801, the island's legislative assembly gained control of the rules governing voting rights but did not change the criteria. It even reiterated the ban on voting by Catholics. Because of the growing number of Irish and Scottish arrivals, Catholics were beginning to outnumber Protestants, even though initially the colony had been intended to receive only Protestant immigrants. It was not until five years later, with a rapid rise in the number of immigrants from the Highlands of Scotland, many of whom were destitute, that the assembly decided to restrict the right to vote. In rural areas, Protestant residents remained eligible to vote if they owned a freehold yielding at least 20 shillings a year, leased land for 40 shillings a year, or occupied and maintained land and paid annual rent of at least £3. In Princetown, Georgetown and Charlottetown, freeholders retained their right to vote, while those who maintained and occupied property, regardless of its value, acquired the same right.

To prevent squatters, labourers and transients from voting, the assembly imposed further financial restrictions in 1830. In future, freeholders in rural areas would have to own property yielding annual revenue of at least 40 shillings, not 20, and individuals occupying and maintaining property would have to be paying an annual rent of £5 (up from £3). Unchanged was the requirement that tenant farmers or leaseholders be paying an annual rent of 40 shillings. Freeholders in Princetown, Georgetown and Charlottetown retained the right to vote, but individuals responsible for maintaining a property had to occupy a building commanding an annual rent of at least £10. In addition, owners of real property producing annual revenue of at least £10 would be eligible to vote.

Before agreeing to the new electoral law, London demanded the removal of all clauses restricting the right to vote to Protestants, thus giving Catholics the vote. Six years later, Prince Edward Island passed a law prohibiting women from voting. This decision was surprising, as there appears to be no evidence that women had sought to exercise this right.

Since the beginning of the nineteenth century, the assembly had been attempting to restrict the electorate by increasing the property requirements, mainly to bypass the Escheat party, which was calling for the lands of absentee owners to be confiscated and resold to those occupying and working the land. During the 1840s, Escheat supporters lost ground to the more moderate Reformers, who eventually achieved responsible government in 1851. Two years later, the assembly adopted a law authorizing the island government to purchase land from consenting landowners for resale in small parcels to their tenants.

Political tensions subsided, and in 1853, the assembly decided to broaden the electorate considerably. This time, the vote was extended to British subjects age 21 or over who had lived on the island at least 12 months before an election and who were subject to the statutory labour law.* As a result, all British subjects between the ages of 21 and 60 who had lived on the island for at least a year became eligible to vote. This was essentially the equivalent of universal male suffrage. In addition, the vote was granted to British subjects over age 21 who owned or had legal title to an urban freehold, or who owned rural or urban property producing annual revenues of at least 40 shillings. In other words, these landowners could vote more than once – in the electoral district where they lived (that is, where they were subject to the statutory labour law) and in the district where they owned property that met the eligibility requirements.

Moreover, like the other colonies of British North America, since 1847 Prince Edward Island had had the authority to enact regulations governing the naturalization of non-British settlers. Nearly all immigrants came from the British Isles and thus were already British subjects. It was not until 1863 that the assembly passed a law granting civil and political rights to non-British arrivals who had lived on the island for at least seven years.

Of the original colonies that formed Canada, Prince Edward Island had the most liberal electoral law when it joined Confederation in 1873, although a sizable fraction of its population was still prohibited from voting: women, anyone over 60 years of age who was not a landowner and immigrants who had been living on the island less than seven years.

Prince Edward Island

1773 First elected assembly. Eligible to vote: all Protestants on the island. There are no legislated restrictions, though convention dictates that women and children do not vote.

1785 Quakers enfranchised and allowed to stand for public office.

1801 Legislative assembly gains control of rules governing right to vote (but does not change them at this time).

1830 Restrictions on voting by non-Protestants removed.

1836 Law passed explicitly limiting the franchise to men.

1851 Responsible government achieved.

1853 The practical equivalent of universal male suffrage introduced.

1862 Elected legislative council secured.

1873 Prince Edward Island joins Confederation with the most liberal electoral law of all the former colonies (only British Columbia's franchise is broader), but significant numbers are still disenfranchised: women, men over age 60 who own no land and non-British arrivals who have lived on the island less than seven years.

Cape Breton: A Colony Without Voters

With the capitulation of the fortress of Louisbourg in July 1758, Île Royale came under the control of the British. Five years later, after the Treaty of Paris, London joined Cape Breton with the colony of Nova Scotia; now Nova Scotia's electoral laws applied to Cape Breton. To reserve the operation of the coal mines and fisheries for the Crown, authorities in England had decided to give residents of Cape Breton occupancy permits, not freeholds. Suddenly, no Cape Breton resident could vote, since only freeholders could vote in Nova Scotia.

By 1763, Cape Breton was still occupied by a handful of Acadians who had evaded deportation.

*This law required men between the ages of 16 and 60 to provide four days' labour (or the cash equivalent) each year for road building and maintenance.

Between then and the end of the American Revolution, however, immigrants from the British Isles, particularly Scotland, settled there. Then, in 1784, several hundred Loyalists arrived in Cape Breton, founding the city of Sydney. The same year, London separated Cape Breton from Nova Scotia, making it a separate colony with its own governor and executive council. No legislative assembly was established, apparently for two reasons. First, the population was deemed to be too poor to support such an institution. Second, the vast majority of Cape Breton's population was made up of Catholic, Gaelic-speaking Scottish settlers and Acadians, also Catholic, who spoke only French. To participate in the proceedings of a house of assembly under the British system of the time, an individual had to speak English and be a non-Catholic.

Cape Breton gradually became fairly prosperous. Early in the nineteenth century, residents began to demand a house of assembly, but London turned a deaf ear. In 1820, with the population of Cape Breton nearing 20,000, London decided to merge it with Nova Scotia again. The annexation occurred shortly after Nova Scotia's assembly had adjourned. As the laws of Nova Scotia did not yet apply to Cape Breton, the governor and his councillors decided who would have the vote in the newly annexed territory.

Giving the vote only to freeholders, as in the rest of Nova Scotia, would be tantamount to denying it to virtually the entire population of Cape Breton, as only a handful of speculators had been granted land under its system of tenure since 1784. Nearly all residents were therefore tenants or tenant farmers, leasing Crown land or land belonging to a land speculator. The governor and council finally decided to give the vote to tenants on Crown land, a decision that was subsequently ratified by the Nova Scotia assembly. Elsewhere in Nova Scotia, Crown land leaseholders would not obtain the right to vote until 1851, some 30 years later.

The people of Cape Breton were thus denied the right to vote for 57 years – from 1763 to 1820 – an unenviable record for a British North American colony.

Cape Breton

1763 Cape Breton is merged with Nova Scotia and becomes subject to its electoral law; no resident can vote, as no freeholds are permitted on Cape Breton, and only freeholders can vote in Nova Scotia.

1784 The colonies are separated again, but no legislative assembly is established.

1820 The colonies are rejoined; tenants on Crown land in Cape Breton gain the vote after 57 years without it.

New Brunswick: A Fragmented Colony

When the British took Louisbourg in 1758, several small Acadian communities lay scattered across the vast territory of New Brunswick. Some, situated along the southern shore of the Baie des Chaleurs, would become towns like Caraquet, Shippegan and Miscou. Others were situated at the mouths of rivers that emptied into the Gulf of St. Lawrence, and still others on the north shore of the Bay of Fundy and in the Saint John Valley. As they had done elsewhere, the British conducted a deportation policy for several years, and, as elsewhere, many Acadians evaded deportation by fleeing to the bush, beyond the reach of English bayonets, particularly along the headwaters of the Saint John River.

In 1763, New Brunswick was merged with Nova Scotia, but the London authorities lost interest in the region. Over the years, several hundred Acadian families returned from exile, while only a few thousand British emigrants settled there, mainly in the Saint John Valley. By the end of the American Revolution, New Brunswick was still very sparsely populated.

The flood of Loyalists into Nova Scotia prompted profound change. The Loyalists dreamed of "a stable, rural society governed by an able tightly knit oligarchy of Loyalist gentry" (*DCB* V, 156), a dream that translated into a profound distrust of the innovative and democratic spirit of the Americans. Nova Scotia's existing population was largely of American origin and took a dim view of the massive influx of Loyalists. In 1784, to ease the political tensions caused by their arrival, London separated the territory of New Brunswick from Nova Scotia to accommodate Loyalist settlement. Between 15,000 and 20,000 Loyalists settled in New Brunswick and were later joined by immigrants of Scottish, Irish and English origin.

Until the mid-nineteenth century and even beyond, colonization of New Brunswick bore little resemblance to that of its sister colonies, Nova Scotia and Prince Edward Island. The colony consisted of a series of separate communities that had very little contact with each other, with the result that settlers in each isolated region were generally unaware of conditions elsewhere but vigorously supported any measure intended to meet their own needs. As a result, businessmen and politicians from the various regions represented conflicting interests and proposed divergent solutions. In this situation, the electorate tends to play a less significant role than when there are political parties promoting a platform or advocating specific measures affecting the population as a whole.

New Brunswick

1785 First elected assembly in New Brunswick. Eligible to vote: white males over the age of 21 who have lived in the colony for at least three months and agree to take an oath of allegiance.

1786 Votes of Catholic Acadians disallowed in a disputed election.

1791 First electoral law adopted – one of the strictest in British North America; receives royal assent in 1795.

1810 Catholics and Jews gain the vote when oath requirement is lifted.

1848 Vote withdrawn from women.

1855 New electoral law extends the franchise to include tradesmen, professionals and senior clerks (in addition to landowners) but still excludes most labourers and workers (who make up some 21 percent of men over the age of 16 in 1861). Voting by secret ballot introduced.

When New Brunswick obtained its status as a colony in 1784, the first governor was given the usual orders: to govern with the advice of his executive council until circumstances favoured establishment of a legislative assembly. In the fall of 1785, the circumstances were favourable. The number of freeholders was extremely small, so the governor gave the right to vote to any white male age 21 or over who had lived in the colony at least three months and who agreed to take the oath of allegiance. But these liberal criteria disappeared in a flash when, the day after the first election, the losing candidate in Westmorland County complained to the legislative assembly

Saint John, 1865

A record dating from 1865 shows the existence of some 20 shipyards in Saint John, New Brunswick, employing 1,267 men at an average wage of $1 a day. As shipbuilding is a seasonal occupation, these workers would have had an annual income of scarcely more than $250 or $300. To be eligible to vote in New Brunswick in 1865, individuals had to earn a minimum of $400 annually.

that he had been defeated by the Acadian vote. In January 1786, the assembly resolved that voting by Roman Catholics had been illegal, being contrary to the laws of England. The assembly then unseated the winning candidate and seated his opponent. In this way, the votes of Acadians were invalidated.

Five years later, the assembly adopted New Brunswick's first electoral law. It also reiterated its January 1786 resolution denying Catholics the vote, enabling sheriffs, who oversaw the elections, to discount the votes of anyone who refused to take the three oaths of state. Once again, Jews found themselves excluded by the same provisions that disenfranchised Catholics.

The requirements of the electoral law were among the strictest of any in the British North American colonies. To be eligible to vote in a given constituency, an individual had to be 21 or older and own property in the riding free of any duties or rents and assessed at £25 or more, or own similar property in another riding assessed at £50 or more. The requirements reflected the conservative mentality of the ruling class in New Brunswick, which had received a large proportion of the Loyalists who had previously held important civilian and military positions in New England. This class was inclined to restrict the vote to major landowners. At the time the law was enacted, a number of settlers owned enough land to be eligible to vote, but a steadily growing number of poorer immigrants swelled the ranks of those ineligible to vote.

These restrictive requirements remained in force for more than half a century, with one exception: in 1810, the assembly did away with the mandatory three oaths, enabling Catholics and Jews to vote. In 1848, however, the Assembly explicitly withdrew the vote from women who met the property requirements. The women's vote had been granted only once before, in the County of Kent in 1830. Had others attempted to have this repeated? From the legislative measure of 1848, it would seem so.

From about the 1820s, in the face of strict eligibility requirements, more and more people took to voting illegally, often going to the polling stations in such large numbers that election officials were unable to verify whether everyone was eligible. Following each general election, the ordinary business of the legislative assembly would often be paralyzed for days, even weeks, because members had to investigate contested elections, an increasingly common phenomenon.

The assembly procrastinated for several decades before adopting a new law in 1855 to extend the franchise. Still eligible to vote were all freeholders owning property assessed at £25 or more; they were joined by anyone whose annual income, combined with the value of his real and personal property, was at least £100. It was still necessary, of course, to be a British subject age 21 or older; a foreigner could obtain this status only after residing in the colony for seven years. In short, this legislation gave the right to vote to almost all property owners and to those in the upper income bracket, but it still excluded the vast majority of labourers and workers. At Confederation, New Brunswick's 1855 electoral law was still in effect.

Lower Canada: A British Colony Unlike the Others

July 1608: Samuel de Champlain founds Quebec. September 1759: Quebec surrenders to the English. In the intervening 150 years, a colony of French-speaking Catholics had put down roots in the St. Lawrence Valley and spread west and south into the land of the Illinois and to Louisiana. This was New France. Compared to its neighbour, New England, New France grew geographically by leaps and bounds; demographically, however, it moved at a snail's pace.

At the turn of the eighteenth century, New France consisted of four main colonies: at the periphery, Newfoundland, Acadia and Louisiana; in the centre, Canada, firmly entrenched in the St. Lawrence Valley but controlling a network of trading and military posts extending to Hudson Bay, the Great Lakes region and the Mississippi Valley. Because of its relatively large population, Canada dominated the rest of New France, but the total population was still only about 14,000. New England, by contrast, huddled along the Atlantic coast between Acadia and Spanish Florida, was already home to some 225,000 settlers.

Under the Treaty of Utrecht, France ceded present-day Nova Scotia, as well as Hudson Bay and Newfoundland, to England in 1713. Fifty years later, under the Treaty of Paris, France ceded the rest of New France. On that date, New England's population was nearly 1.5 million, while Canada's was only about 60,000. That population had already developed characteristics that distinguished it from its neighbours to the south, however, who had remained closer to their European roots.

Within two generations, the French settlers in the St. Lawrence Valley had become "Canadianized," blending their European heritage with traits borrowed from the Aboriginal world. Aware that they enjoyed far more freedom than their counterparts in France, they referred to themselves as *habitants* rather than *paysans*. Driven by a spirit of egalitarianism, they usually proved resistant to hierarchy. They were commonly called "Canadians" to distinguish them from French sojourners in the colony who had not joined settler society. The colonial authorities – civilian, military and religious alike – complained regularly of the rebellious spirit of the Canadians.

In 1752, a French military engineer visiting Canada, like many other chroniclers of the time, was struck by their profound sense of independence: "Canadians generally are unruly, stubborn and act only according to their fancy and whim ...". (Franquet, 103, translation) In short, the French of the St. Lawrence Valley became Canadianized before the English of New England became Americanized, and this distinction became more pronounced over time.

In 1763, England was convinced, mistakenly, that it was inheriting a French society. English authorities did not fully understand the reality: that

Lower Canada 1815–1850

Between 1815 and 1850 in the city of Québec, a day labourer working 20 days a month earned no more than £12 or £13 a year, and the purchase of a large loaf of bread cost him nearly 40 percent of his daily earnings. With such an income, day labourers, who accounted for about 15 to 20 percent of workers in Québec, certainly could not afford the luxury of voting.

Lower Canada, 1821

In 1821, there were 468 tenants in Saint-Roch, a suburb of Québec inhabited mainly by artisans, day labourers and construction workers. Rents were quite low in Saint-Roch, and two thirds of housing fell below the average annual rental of £11. As a result, a corresponding two thirds of tenants could not vote, as a tenant had to be paying an annual rent of £10 to be eligible to vote.

the former subjects of the king of France already formed a distinct people, more North American than European, and wanted to remain that way. By the *Royal Proclamation of 1763*, issued by George III, Canada became the Province of Quebec, and its first governor received the usual orders to call a legislative assembly when conditions allowed. This might be surprising at first glance, but less so when considered in light of the fact that London anticipated a strong influx of Protestant settlers from New England, who would quickly assimilate the Canadians.

In the meantime, a major problem arose in 1764: the legal status of Canadians. Colonial authorities sought the opinion of legal experts, who finally declared that the conquered people were not subject to the "Incapacities, Disabilities and Penalties" imposed upon Catholics in England. (*DCB* IV, xli)

Two years after the Royal Proclamation, only a few hundred English, mostly merchants and traders, had settled in the new colony, mainly in Québec and Montréal – nowhere near the influx expected. In late 1767, the governor was forced to note that, barring some "unforeseeable disaster," the numerical superiority of Canadians, far from diminishing, would increase. London therefore decided to revise its policy and, among other things, gave up the idea of permitting a legislative assembly. But the Canadians paid little attention, accustomed as they were to living by a precept common under the French regime: "Chacun parle en son nom et personne au nom de tous." ("Each one speaks on his own behalf and no one on behalf of everyone.")

Under the *Quebec Act* of 1774, the Province of Quebec was to be administered by a governor and an executive council. The act also reinstated the *Coutume de Paris* as the civil code, replacing the common law, and retained the seigneurial system. But 10 years later, the "unforeseeable disaster" occurred: a wave of Anglo-Protestant settlers, in the form of several thousand Loyalists, flooded the colony.

It was not a very big wave: some 10,000 to 15,000 immigrants. All the same, it was enough to shift the demographic balance; the English minority jumped from 4 or 5 percent of the total population to between 10 and 15 percent. Some took up residence on the southeast shore of the Gaspé peninsula or in the Eastern Townships, but most settled north of Lake Ontario. The Loyalists wanted neither the seigneurial system nor the *Coutume de Paris*; they demanded English civil law, the English system of land tenure and parliamentary institutions. London was forced to pay attention.

The *Constitutional Act* of 1791 established a new colony north of the Great Lakes: Upper Canada. The Province of Quebec became Lower Canada, retaining the *Coutume de Paris* and the seigneurial system. The act also established the English land tenure system wherever land had not yet been transferred under the seigneurial system, notably in the Eastern Townships. Finally, to satisfy the British minority in Lower Canada, London agreed to a house of assembly.

Having done this, however, colonial authorities could not restrict the vote to English-speaking settlers. The *Constitutional Act* therefore stipulated that anyone age 21 or older who had not been convicted of a serious criminal offence or treason, and who was a British subject by birth or had become one when Canada was ceded to England, was entitled to vote if he had the necessary property qualifications. In rural areas, this meant owning

Montréal, 1825

With its population of 22,540, Montréal was the most populous city in British North America in 1825. There were 2,698 assessed properties in the area, 2,085 of which were in the suburbs and 613 in the city. While the average revenue from these properties was £33, revenues could be as high as £82 in the city or as low as £18 in the suburbs. In the suburbs, some 522 properties earned only a modest £6 annually, well below the £10 annual rent a tenant had to be paying to be eligible to vote.

land yielding at least 40 shillings a year, less any rent or charges owing. In urban areas, this meant owning a lot with a habitable dwelling generating annual revenue of at least £5, less any rent or charges owing; tenants paying an annual rent of at least £10 were also eligible to vote. The act also stipulated that property conferring the right to vote could be owned or held under an occupancy permit issued by the governor and executive council.

Unlike women in the other British North American colonies, women in Lower Canada who met the property requirements could vote. Nothing in the *Constitutional Act* prevented them from doing so, and they were not subject to English common law. They therefore took to voting, apparently without arousing comment, until a tragic event altered the electoral landscape. During a by-election held in Montréal between April 25 and May 22, 1832, illegalities and acts of intimidation and violence occurred almost daily. On the 22nd day of voting, the authorities asked the army to intervene. The result: three Canadians shot dead by British soldiers.

Until then, the Reformers, led by Louis-Joseph Papineau, had supported women's right to vote; but they had a change of heart, believing that polling stations had become too dangerous for "the weaker sex." In 1834, the house of assembly adopted a law depriving women of the right to vote. Because of a legal technicality, however, London rejected the act, and the women of Lower Canada retained the right to vote.

The electorate of Lower Canada, as defined by the *Constitutional Act* of 1791, was not altered between then and the creation of the Province of Canada through the union of Upper and Lower Canada in 1840. Political life in Lower Canada proceeded along essentially the same lines as in the other colonies of British North America: reform-oriented parties that demanded major political change opposed conservative parties more satisfied with the status quo. In Lower Canada, however, unlike elsewhere, the struggle among political parties was played out against a cultural backdrop: reformers promoted the interests of French-speaking Canadians, while conservatives advanced those of the English-speaking minority. As a result, Lower Canada was a British colony quite unlike the others.

In 1810, Governor James Craig complained bitterly, as officials of the French regime had done before him, about Canadians' spirit of independence and insubordination. He wrote, "It seems to be a favorite object with them to be considered as a separate Nation; *la Nation canadienne* is their constant expression." (Ryerson 1973, 45) And following the rebellion of 1837–1838, Lord Durham in turn noted:

> I expected to find a contest between a government and a people: I found two nations warring in the bosom of a single state: I found a struggle, not of principles, but of races ... The circumstances of the early colonial administration excluded the native Canadian from power, and vested all offices of trust and emolument in the hands of strangers of English origin.
>
> *Cornell et al., 211–212*

Then the man known among his contemporaries as Radical Jack because of his liberal ideas concluded:

> There can hardly be conceived a nationality more destitute of all that can invigorate and elevate a people, than that which is

exhibited by the descendants of the French in Lower Canada, owing to their retaining their peculiar language and manners. They are a people with no history, and no literature.

Cornell et al., 214

Lower Canada was definitely a British colony like no other.

Upper Canada: The Era of the Family Compact

Established by the *Constitutional Act* of 1791, Upper Canada inherited the same rules as Lower Canada for determining its voters. Yet these rules were not applied in quite the same way because Upper Canada, a colony founded specifically for the Loyalists, inherited common law rather than French civil law. Thus, from the outset, women were excluded from the electorate. Also excluded were members of certain religious sects, such as the Quakers (members of the Society of Friends, who were relatively numerous in Upper Canada), Mennonites, Moravians and Tunkers, as their faiths forbade them from taking an oath. Under common law, an election officer or even a candidate for election could require a voter to take an oath of allegiance before casting a vote. This restriction would not be lifted until 1833, by an act of the British Parliament.

Of all the eligibility criteria, however, the one concerning the definition of a British subject posed the most serious problem. It even started a kind of family quarrel among immigrants from the United States that would last several decades.

When the *Constitutional Act* came into force, some 10,000 Loyalists were living in Upper Canada. At the same time, westward migration in the United States was spilling over into territory north of the Great Lakes, where the authorities were offering Americans land free of charge or for a nominal sum. Over the years, immigrants from the United States flowed steadily into Upper Canada.

Upper and Lower Canada

1791 *Constitutional Act* establishes Upper and Lower Canada and sets voting rules. Eligible to vote: British subjects over 21 who have not been convicted of a serious criminal offence or treason and meet property ownership requirements. In Lower Canada, women have the vote, but in Upper Canada, the common law prevails, and women are excluded.

1792 First elected assemblies in Upper and Lower Canada.

1832 Election violence in Montréal results in three deaths.

1834 Polling stations deemed too dangerous for women; legislative assembly of Lower Canada adopts law denying them the vote; London disallows the law.

1840 *Act of Union* unites Upper and Lower Canada as the Province of Canada. Franchise remains as in *Constitutional Act* of 1791.

1841 First elected assembly in the Province of Canada.

1844–1858 Successive measures exclude from voting judges, bankruptcy commissioners, customs officials, imperial tax collectors, paid election agents, court clerks and officers, registrars, sheriffs and their deputies, Crown clerks and assistant clerks, Crown land agents, election officials.

1848 Responsible government in the Province of Canada.

1849 Legislative Assembly of the Province of Canada standardizes electoral law of Upper and Lower Canada.

1853 First electoral law ordering preparation of electoral lists from property assessment rolls; measure abandoned in 1855, after lists remain unfinished; adopted again in 1859, after election fraud becomes widespread.

1861 First election held using registers (lists) of electors compiled through municipal assessment system.

Campaigning, 1862-Style
Before the advent of public street lighting, torchlight parades were popular election events. This one, captured in a wood engraving, was held to honour George Brown, Reform politician and publisher and editor of *The Globe*, the Toronto weekly he founded in 1844. The parade took place in Toronto on December 26, 1862.

These new settlers, unlike their predecessors, were not Loyalists and tended to support the Reformers in large numbers, whereas the Loyalists tended to favour the Conservatives.

In 1800, the Conservatives, who controlled the legislative assembly, started to become alarmed at the situation and passed a measure to the effect that, to be eligible to vote, immigrants from the United States had to have lived in Upper Canada for seven years and have taken an oath of allegiance to the British Crown. In 1804, the Reformers won a majority in the assembly and tried to repeal the measure of 1800, but in vain. The legislative council, controlled by the Conservatives, opposed the move.

Repeated efforts by the Reformers became even more futile after an event eight years later. On June 18, 1812, the president of the United States declared war on England. The population of Upper Canada was by then close to 94,000. Eighty percent of the population was of American origin, but less than a quarter of them were of Loyalist descent. When the American army tried to invade Upper Canada, the Loyalists and British settlers defended the territory, but most non-Loyalists remained neutral. This no doubt aroused the distrust of other Upper Canadians, and because the Conservatives still controlled the legislature, the Reformers' efforts continued to be frustrated.

From 1815 on, a steadily mounting number of immigrants from the British Isles chose Upper Canada as their destination. As British subjects, they had the vote, provided they met the property requirements. This time, fearing a loss of political control, the old colonists of American origin – Loyalists and non-Loyalists alike – joined forces. In 1821, the assembly decreed that an occupancy permit issued by the lieutenant-governor of Upper Canada was insufficient to obtain the vote.

Consulted on this point, legal experts in London concurred with the assembly's pronouncement. In their view, the *Constitutional Act* of 1791 was explicit: only an occupancy permit granted by the governor of Lower Canada could confer the right to vote. The governor had not granted such permits since the first general election, leaving this task to the lieutenant-governor. In addition, because it had become increasingly difficult since 1818 for immigrants to obtain a freehold, "annual batches of poor" (Ryerson 1968, 27) from the British Isles were swelling the ranks of the disenfranchised. Throughout the 1830s, settlers of British origin outnumbered even those of American origin, with the result that a sizable portion of the population of Upper Canada had no electoral voice.

In the meantime, the squabble among Upper Canadians of American origin died down. In 1828, with London's consent, the assembly adopted a law stating that foreigners who had settled in Upper Canada before 1820 would automatically become British subjects. The same act stipulated, moreover, that foreigners who had come to Upper Canada between 1820 and March 1, 1828, could obtain the status of British subject after living in the colony for seven years and taking an oath of allegiance. This act superseded the 1800 law.

Rival Candidates, 1828
At Perth, Upper Canada, Alex Thom, William Morris (who was re-elected) and election officials survey the crowd from the "hustings." Originally the platform on which candidates were nominated for the British Parliament, the hustings was where Canadian voters had to stand and declare their electoral choices before the advent of the secret ballot (1874). Now the term is synonymous with the campaign trail. (Watercolour by F. H. Consett)

In short, on the eve of the union of the Canadas, the criteria for voting in Upper Canada had become considerably more restrictive than those in force in Lower Canada, even though those criteria had originally derived from the same legislation. Why? Reformer William Lyon Mackenzie denounced the culprit in plain terms in 1833:

> This family compact surround the Lieutenant Governor, and mould him, like wax, to their will; they fill every office with their relatives, dependants and partisans; by them justices of the peace and officers of the militia are made and unmade; … the whole of the revenues of Upper Canada are in reality at their mercy; – they are Paymasters, Receivers, Auditors, King, Lords and Commons!
>
> *Ryerson 1973, 93*

Following his investigation of 1838, Lord Durham also did not mince words:

> In the preceding account of … Lower Canada, I have described the effect which the irresponsibility of the real advisers of the Governor had in lodging permanent authority in the hands of a powerful party … But in none of the North American Provinces has this exhibited itself for so long a period or to such an extent, as in Upper Canada, which has long been entirely governed by a party commonly designated throughout the Province as the "family compact" … For a long time this body of men … possessed almost all the highest public offices, by means of which, and of its influence in the Executive Council, it wielded all the powers of government; it maintained influence in the legislature by means of its predominance in the Legislative Council …
>
> *Cornell et al., 212*

In short, the Family Compact effectively transformed Upper Canada into an oligarchy.

A Right in Jeopardy

Lord Durham was given the task of identifying the causes of political unrest in the colonies of British North America and proposing solutions. His first recommendation was to give each colony responsible government – an idea London did not accept until some 10 years later. Radical Jack also proposed a second solution aimed at the one colony decidedly unlike the others – Lower Canada. Here, according to Durham's diagnosis, the political problem was coupled with a cultural one. His solution could not have been simpler: to subjugate one of the two cultural groups to the other. The means also could not have been simpler: uniting Lower Canada with Upper Canada. Mathematically, Durham was quite right: every year since the end of the Napoleonic Wars, immigrants had been leaving the British Isles by the thousands to improve their lot in North America, while the inhabitants of Lower Canada could now depend only on themselves to increase their numbers. Durham calculated:

> If the population of Upper Canada is rightly estimated at 400,000, the English inhabitants of Lower Canada at 150,000,

and the French at 450,000, the union of the two Provinces would not only give a clear English majority, but one which would be increased every year by the influence of English emigration; and I have little doubt that the French, when once placed, by the legitimate course of events and the working of natural causes, in a minority, would abandon their vain hopes of nationality …

Cornell et al., 214

The following warning accompanied Durham's recommendation:

I am averse to every plan that has been proposed for giving an equal number of members to the two Provinces, in order to attain the temporary end of out-numbering the French, because I think the same object will be obtained without any violation of the principles of representation, and without any such appearance of injustice …

Cornell et al., 214

London finally accepted Durham's recommendation for unification and created the Province of Canada from the two provinces: Canada East, still commonly known as Lower Canada, and Canada West, or Upper Canada. But London ignored Durham's warning and gave each province the same number of representatives, even though Lower Canada had 150,000 more inhabitants than its neighbour. This measure would bear out Durham's prediction: it would tend to "defeat the purposes of union, and perpetuate the ideas of disunion." (Cornell et al., 214)

Annual Pay of Country Schoolteachers, British North America, 1848

	Male Schoolteachers	Female Schoolteachers	Comments
Upper Canada	£30	£15	Without lodging
Lower Canada	£36	£18	Without lodging
Nova Scotia	£38-8s	£19-4s	With food and lodging
New Brunswick	£40	£20	Without lodging

With such low annual incomes, it would be surprising if even one country schoolteacher was eligible to vote in British North America in 1848, since in rural areas, individuals had to own property of a certain value to be eligible to vote.

All that remained was to have the union approved by the population affected, a task London entrusted to the governor general of British North America, Lord Sydenham, a highly ambitious and self-assured man – "the greatest coxcomb I ever saw, and the vainest dog," as one of his contemporaries wrote in his personal journal. (*DCB* VII, 855) Sydenham soon realized that the success of his

Vote for no man whose conduct in private and public life is not above suspicion, and inquire with due diligence before you give your suffrages.

– William Lyon Mackenzie
Address to the reformers of Upper Canada
Toronto, September 1834

mission depended on the election of a group of representatives supportive of the new regime. In Lower Canada, the largely French-Canadian population unanimously opposed the union, while in Upper Canada, ultra-Conservatives and extremist Reformers opposed it as well. But Sydenham knew that, under the terms of the act, the governor had the power to set the boundaries for certain ridings, appoint returning officers, select the location of polling stations and set the election date. Moreover, as governor, Sydenham was also commander-in-chief of the army and head of government. He was certainly not the type of person to trouble himself with scruples; in his view, the end justified the means.

Beginning in early 1840, he did everything possible to win the forthcoming election. "He plans and talks of nothing else," wrote his secretary. (Abella, 328) In Upper Canada, Sydenham acted like a party leader, naming most of the candidates he wanted to see elected. He made promises or threats, depending on the circumstances. For example, to persuade them to withdraw, he offered government positions to two candidates campaigning for votes in Bytown. He also threatened to deprive voters of government grants if his candidate was defeated. He called on officials to back his supporters and appointed returning officers dedicated to his cause. By the fall of 1840, Sydenham was assured of a victory in Upper Canada. In mid-October, the Toronto *Herald* reproduced the list of 26 candidates who were also government employees and concluded, "His Excellency should nominate the whole of the members and not beguile us with 'shadows of a free election'." (Abella, 332)

In Lower Canada, where he could hope to see only a few candidates elected, Sydenham resorted

Allies in Reform

Robert Baldwin (*left*) and Louis-Hippolyte La Fontaine (*right*) were partners in the struggle to make governments responsible to the elected assembly. La Fontaine had been imprisoned briefly in 1838 for his active nationalism, while Baldwin belonged to Upper Canada's landed gentry. But both men considered the 1840 *Act of Union* unjust to French Canada, and they became friends and political allies. (Lithographs, 1848)

NOTICE.

LOUIS H. LA FONTAINE, ESQ.,

Accompanied by Dr. Baldwin,

WILL MEET THE FREEHOLDERS,

FRIENDLY TO HIS ELECTION,

For the North Riding of the County of York, at

THE FOLLOWING TIMES AND PLACES.

At Sharon**--On Monday, 6th September, at noon.**
At Bennett's, in North Gwillimbury**--Tuesday, 7th, at do**
At Johnson's Mills, in Georgina**--Wednesday, 8th, at do**
At Uxbridge Village**--Thursday, 9th, at do**
At Stouffville**--Friday, 10th, at do.**

Election Literature, 1841
Robert Baldwin, advocate of responsible government and a bicultural nation, supported the bid of fellow Reformer Louis-Hippolyte La Fontaine for a Toronto-area seat in the legislature of the newly created Province of Canada (uniting Upper and Lower Canada). When the Province of Canada won responsible government in 1848, La Fontaine became its premier.

to other ploys. He shamelessly readjusted the boundaries of urban ridings. He cut off the mainly French-Canadian suburbs from ridings in the cities of Québec, Montréal and Trois-Rivières, keeping only the downtown English-dominated cores. Nearly all voters in the suburbs were thus deprived of the vote, since in the rural ridings to which the suburbs were now attached, tenants did not yet have the vote. To increase the anglophone vote in Sherbrooke, Sydenham added on the neighbouring town of Lennoxville. By this single boundary change alone, the governor guaranteed the election of six of his candidates in a community where he had previously been assured of just one seat.

In each rural riding, Sydenham set up a single polling station, located not in the centre of the riding but at the perimeter and, where possible, in an English enclave. For example, in the riding of Terrebonne, the polling station was set up at New Glasgow, a small Irish and Scottish community at the northern extremity of the riding, a few days' travel from its centre, which had a strong French-Canadian majority. The same tactic was used in several other ridings, including Ottawa, Chambly and Berthier. Finally, by holding the election in early March, a time of year when the roads were virtually impassable, Sydenham could count on a low turnout among the French-Canadian electorate.

Not content with all these pre-election schemes, the governor intervened in the election itself. In Kingston, on the third day of voting, he dismissed an official named Robert Berrie, who the day before had voted against Sydenham's candidate. The other officials quickly got the message; most supported the governor, and the rest abstained from voting. In some ridings where the vote was close, such as London, the governor had land patents granted *in extremis* to his supporters but not to his opponents, thus ensuring victory. In the ridings of Beauharnois, Vaudreuil, Chambly, Bonaventure, Rouville, Montréal and Terrebonne, he sent gangs of ruffians armed with clubs and guns to take over the polling stations and prevent his opponents from voting. The toll: one dead in Montréal, two in Vaudreuil and three in Beauharnois. In Terrebonne, to avoid a bloodbath, the French-Canadian Reform leader Louis-Hippolyte La Fontaine withdrew his candidacy. Riots broke out in Upper Canada, and there were deaths in Toronto and in the counties of Durham and Halton West.

As commander-in-chief of the army, Sydenham did not hesitate to use the army for his own ends. He refused to send troops to protect 15 opposition candidates who sought protection, while granting the same protection to any of his supporters who requested it.

Through these and other underhanded tactics, Sydenham managed to win the election. In June 1841, he wrote proudly to Lord Russell, "I have gained a most complete victory. I shall carry the measures I want." (Abella, 343) He did not savour his victory for long, however, as illness forced him to resign a month later. Lord Sydenham certainly did not invent election strong-arm tactics, but he used them to an extent never seen before. After his departure, election morals continued to decline in the Province of Canada. In this regard, the Canada of 1867 inherited an unenviable legacy.

The Province of Canada: Changing Rules Reflect Instability

In 1840, the Province of Canada entered a period of political unrest that would intensify from the mid-1850s on, resulting eventually in an impasse some 10 years later. One of the causes of this unrest was equal representation, which initially worked to Upper Canada's advantage and then soon worked against it. As early as 1850, the population of Upper Canada exceeded that of Lower Canada because of the heavy flow of immigrants. Ironically, what had been fair in 1840, when English Canadians were in the minority, became unfair in 1850, when they were in the majority.

Beginning in the early 1850s, Reformers in Upper Canada, led by *Globe* editor George Brown, demanded representation by population. Over the years, this demand gained popular support and played an important role during elections. At the same time, with the advent of responsible government, many assembly members adhered to the double majority rule: the government had to have a majority not only in the Province of Canada as a whole, but in each of the component colonies as well.

At first, this rule posed no problem, since the Reformers, soon to be called Liberals, held sway in both provinces. But in 1854, Lower Canada elected the Liberals while Upper Canada voted in the Conservatives. A coalition government was formed, made up of members from both parties. But this type of government was precarious, as its survival depended on a few moderate members who switched allegiance according to circumstances. In the years that followed, one coalition government after another fell, until the government machinery finally jammed in 1864. The system failed; it no longer truly met the needs of the people. Three years later, there would be a new constitutional compromise: Confederation.

The political uncertainty inherent in the Union was reflected in electoral law. During its brief life – just over a quarter of a century – the Province of Canada passed no fewer than four major election laws affecting the right to vote, as well as numerous other subsidiary acts and regulations that either restricted or expanded the electorate.

From Political Prisoner to MP
Louis Lacoste, a notary public from Boucherville, Quebec, was 40 when Jean-Joseph Girouard did this charcoal sketch. A political activist since 1834, Lacoste had been imprisoned in 1837–1838 for his support of the Patriots, but he later won a seat in Parliament, defeating Alexandre-Édouard Kierzkowski in an 1861 by-election (see page 7). Lacoste held the seat until Confederation, when he was appointed to the Senate.

There is no inalienable right in any man to exercise the franchise.

– Sir John A. Macdonald
Parliamentary debates on Confederation
1865

Initially, the *Act of Union* in no way altered the eligibility criteria; it simply upheld those of the *Constitutional Act* of 1791. In time, however, these criteria underwent various changes in Upper and Lower Canada. In 1849, the Province of Canada passed a law intended to standardize the electoral law of Upper and Lower Canada. In rural ridings, British subjects age 21 or older who owned a freehold or land under the seigneurial system with an annual revenue, less charges, of 40 shillings were still entitled to vote. In urban ridings, owners of a plot of land with a dwelling yielding a net annual revenue of £5 could also vote, provided they were British subjects at least 21 years old. Tenants had the same right, provided they had lived in the city for the 12 months preceding an election and had paid an annual rent of £10.

On the face of it, this law reinstated the property requirements of the *Constitutional Act*, with one exception: in rural ridings, it no longer covered owners of property held through a permit issued by the governor. In urban ridings, the qualifications may have been held over from the early part of the century strictly for the sake of appearances: since the 1820s, there had been a general decline in the economic standing of labourers, artisans and workers, with the result that an annual rent of £10 in 1850 was proportionately higher than in 1800. Finally, the 1849 act prohibited women from voting – the result of a complaint by a defeated candidate in Halton West (Upper Canada) in an election four years earlier. The candidate protested that seven of the votes counted for his opponent had been from women, contrary to common law. The upshot was that women in Lower Canada, who had been able to vote since 1791 under French civil law, well and truly lost this right.

Also in 1849, the Province of Canada enacted legislation concerning voting by foreigners; it stipulated that all foreigners residing in the colony at the time of Union would now be considered British subjects and could exercise their political rights. Foreign immigrants who had come to the colony after Union could obtain the same status if they remained for seven years and agreed to take the oath of allegiance.

A new elections act affecting voters was adopted in 1853. In rural ridings, all British subjects age 21 or older could vote if they were on the assessment rolls as landowners, tenants or occupants of a property worth £50 or more or generating annual revenues of at least £5. In urban ridings, anyone whose name appeared on the assessment roll as a landowner, tenant or occupant of a property generating annual revenues of at least £7 and 10 shillings acquired the right to vote. This legislation was accompanied by a new measure: the preparation of electoral lists from property assessment rolls. The new qualifications became mandatory for all of Upper Canada and for the cities of Québec and Montréal; elsewhere in Lower Canada, they remained optional, as very few municipalities had assessment rolls.

While this law expanded the categories of voters, taking in tenants and occupants in rural ridings and occupants in urban ridings, it was still restrictive, as it raised the qualifications appreciably. In rural areas, it jumped by 250 percent, while in urban ridings, it rose by 150 percent. Moreover, the gap between the rural and urban qualifications was tending to narrow, an obvious indication of growing urbanization.

The next year, on the very eve of the 1853 act coming into force, the government found that there were still no electoral lists for Lower Canada and only a few for Upper Canada. It therefore passed a provisional act, extending the time allotted to prepare the lists by one year. This law made use of the qualifications established in the previous year's act optional in both provinces. But by 1855, compilation of the electoral lists still remained largely unfinished; the government therefore decided to make the provisional law of 1854 permanent but gave up the idea of electoral lists. To avoid fraud resulting from the absence of lists, the government introduced a multitude of oaths. But in fact, the act soon proved unenforceable.

In 1859 – after an election in which so many false oaths were sworn that in some ridings, the number of votes cast was as much as triple the number of eligible voters – the government decided to remedy the situation. The assembly adopted the fourth elections act in less than 10 years. The new law returned to the provisions of the 1853 act and abolished once and for all the optional revenue requirement of 40 shillings in rural areas. Again it became mandatory in both provinces to compile electoral lists from the assessment rolls. In rural areas, the vote was given only to British subjects age 21 or older who owned, leased or occupied landed property assessed at $200 or more or generating annual revenues of at least $20; in urban areas, the same categories of individuals had the vote, provided their property was assessed at $300 or generated annual revenues of at least $30.* In the same year, 1859, the residency period required of foreigners to become British subjects was reduced to three years.

But in Upper Canada, some considered these qualifications too permissive, believing that they extended the franchise too far down the social ladder. In 1866, the government decided to change the way property assessment was done in Upper Canada, while increasing the property requirements for voting. Only landowners and occupants of property assessed at $600 in cities, $400 in towns, $300 in incorporated villages and $200 in townships could vote. In ridings where workers were numerous, this measure eliminated eligibility for many voters – more than 300 in the county of London, for example, and about 900 in Hamilton.

Along with the several elections acts, the government adopted a series of statutory measures designed to exclude from the vote persons who, by their position, exerted some influence in society. Thus, between 1844 and 1858, members of a number of groups – no doubt because they were thought to exercise a degree of influence in society – successively lost the right to vote; they included judges, bankruptcy commissioners, customs officials, imperial tax collectors, paid election agents, court clerks and officers, registrars, sheriffs and their deputies, Crown clerks and assistant Crown clerks, Crown land agents and all election officials.

These were the statutes in force at Confederation. The same categories of voters existed in both parts of the Province of Canada, but the property requirements were higher in Upper Canada than in Lower Canada.

British Columbia: The Importance of Being English

When it was founded in 1849, the colony of Vancouver Island had virtually no independent settlers; it was still just a fur trading post inhabited by employees of the Hudson's Bay Company. Under the circumstances, the governor felt obliged not only to postpone election of an assembly indefinitely,

*In effect, this was the same qualification as in 1853, but expressed in dollars instead of pounds sterling following a change in the currency system.

British Columbia

1856 British North America's smallest legislative assembly (seven members) is established on Vancouver Island and meets after an election in which about 40 people voted. Eligible to vote: freeholders with at least 20 acres.

1863 First election for one third of the members of a legislative council (other two thirds appointed by the Crown); each electoral district sets its own criteria for voting eligibility.

1866 Vancouver Island joins British Columbia. At next election, no voting restrictions on the mainland except in New Westminster, where Chinese and Aboriginal people are excluded. Island districts allow voting only by landowners who are British subjects and meet three-month residency test.

1868 Governor extends New Westminster rules to island districts.

1870 London imposes restrictions on entire colony: eligibility restricted to male British subjects age 21 or older who can read and write English. Excludes Aboriginal people and immigrants of American origin.

1871 Voters approve joining Confederation. Just before British Columbia does so, new restrictions are added: six-month residency rule, minimum property requirements and no taxes owing.

but to administer the colony without the aid of a council. In subsequent years, only a few dozen colonists came to settle there, but in London's eyes, this did not matter: democracy carried obligations. In 1856, the secretary of state for the colonies ordered the governor to call an elected assembly. He was instructed to allow all freeholders with at least 20 acres to vote, including absentee landowners, who could vote through their agents living on the land. In August of the same year, after the colony's 40-odd electors had voted, the seven members of the smallest legislative assembly in the history of British North America held their first session.

In 1859, it was decided that new eligibility criteria were needed to increase the number of voters. However, the presence nearby of a band of adventurers, panning for gold in the Fraser River, prompted conservatism on the part of the legislature, which gave the vote to male British subjects age 21 or older who had lived in the colony for four months and who met at least one of the following conditions: ownership of 20 acres of land; ownership, for three months or more, of property assessed at £50; six months' occupancy of property generating annual rent of £12 or more; 12 months farming 20 acres of farmland as a sharecropper for at least one quarter of the crop; or the practice of surgery, medicine or law, or possession of a diploma from a British college or university. These selection criteria would still be in use when Vancouver Island joined British Columbia in 1866.

In 1857, the discovery of gold on land controlled by the Hudson's Bay Company prompted London to establish a new colony to protect its jurisdiction there. In August 1858, the territory of New Caledonia became a Crown colony known as British Columbia. More than 10,000 prospectors were already sifting feverishly through the gold-bearing sands along the Fraser River. They came mainly from the United States, but also from virtually every country in Europe. As they were a transient population, London postponed establishing parliamentary institutions in British Columbia.

In the meantime, in the hope of attracting British immigrants, land was sold cheap, but only to British subjects. In 1863, the authorities deemed that there were enough British colonists to warrant representative institutions for the colony. However, to ensure that the settled population outweighed the transient population, which had grown during the 1858 and 1862 gold rushes, the governor proposed to set up a legislative council with two thirds of its membership appointed by the Crown and the other third elected by the people. London agreed.

For the first election, the governor subdivided the territory into a number of electoral districts and allowed the residents of each district to define their own criteria for eligibility to vote. The citizens of the district of New Westminster decided that voters would have to be British subjects and have lived in the district at least three months; voters also had to own a freehold assessed at £20 or more, lease property for an annual rent of at least £12 or own land, freehold or by pre-emptive right, assessed at £20 or more. Two other districts, Douglas and Lillooet, adopted the same rules. In the other, more remote districts, there were no restrictions: anyone who wanted to could vote. The situation remained unchanged until Vancouver Island joined British Columbia in November 1866, a union prompted by the end of the gold rush.

The colonial government then decided to abolish the legislative assembly of Vancouver Island and retain the legislative council, extending it to include the new part of the colony. For the first election, the voter selection criteria varied from one electoral district to another. The three districts on Vancouver Island kept the rules established in the 1859 act, when the island was a separate colony. In the mainland districts, there were no voting restrictions. Only the district of New Westminster again took the initiative of setting conditions for exercise of the vote, though these were less restrictive than in 1863: voters had to have lived in the district for three months and be neither Chinese nor "Indian." In the other districts, anyone who wished to could vote.

Smallest Legislature

As a colony separate from British Columbia, Vancouver Island elected its own legislative assembly. At the first election in 1856, some 40 voters elected seven members to North America's smallest legislature. (Painting by Charles Walter Simpson for a book celebrating the Diamond Jubilee of Confederation)

In 1868, on the eve of another election, the governor decided that the rules in force in the district of New Westminster would also apply to the Vancouver Island districts. Two years later, it was London that imposed restrictions on the right to vote, applicable to the entire colony: the vote was restricted to male British subjects age 21 years or older who could read and write English. These conditions, particularly the last one, ruled out Aboriginal people (who constituted at least half the population), while the need to be a British subject excluded a large segment of the population of American origin. London imposed these restrictions on the eve of a referendum-style vote on whether British Columbia should join Confederation, clearly with a view to assuring British Columbia's approval.

The plan succeeded. In 1871, just before joining Confederation, British Columbia introduced further restrictions on the vote: to exercise the right, voters had to have been born British subjects, be at least 21 years of age, be able to read English and have lived in the colony for at least six months. They also had to own a freehold with a net value of $250 or a leasehold producing net annual revenues of $40, or occupy a dwelling generating net annual revenues of $40. Those who held a duly registered pre-emptive title on 100 acres of land or a duly registered mining licence could also vote. The same privilege was accorded to those who paid $40 or more annually for housing or $200 annually for room and board. In addition to meeting the conditions just outlined, the names of prospective voters had to have been published on an electoral list, and any taxes owing to the province had to be paid before a vote could be cast. Finally, the law prohibited from voting anyone convicted of treason or other serious crimes, unless they had been pardoned for the offence or had completed their sentence. Judges, police personnel and returning officers were treated the same way as criminals – they were deprived of the vote while in office.

Voters and Confederation

Ottawa, June 1864. All was not well. In less than four months, two successive governments had come to grief in the Province of Canada. No coalition government could rally or keep a large enough majority to establish its authority. To resolve the impasse, the leaders of the several political factions agreed to form a government whose first task would be to amend the constitution. One solution had been on the drawing board for several years: federating the various British colonies of North America. This solution would kill two birds with one stone: it would resolve the chronic political crisis in the Province of Canada and settle another problem, one of a financial nature.

Since 1850, British North America had been caught up in a frenzy of railway construction, particularly in the Province of Canada. Since 1857, however, Canada had had trouble paying the interest on money borrowed to pay for its railway system. Worse yet, the 2,000 miles of railway lines laid by 1860 – there had been just 66 miles a decade earlier – were not generating enough revenue to cover operating costs or interest on the borrowed capital. With federation of the British colonies, the railway system could be extended *a mari usque ad mare*, thus making it profitable. Another important advantage of a federation: it would stifle public objections in England to excess government spending on the military defence of the North American colonies.

Negotiations eventually dragged on for nine years, until 1873, when the last founding colony joined the federation. Unlike previous constitutions, Confederation was mainly the work of colonial politicians and businessmen, backed by a number of important London financiers and administrators. The plan was essentially drawn up in secret and without input from the electorate. John A. Macdonald, the plan's chief architect, did not hide his aversion to popular consultation. As he put it, "As it would be obviously absurd to submit the complicated details of such a measure to the people, it is not proposed to seek their sanction before asking the Imperial Government to introduce a Bill in the British Parliament." (Ryerson 1973, 354)

Delegates from the several colonies met in September 1864 in Charlottetown and again the next month in Québec, both times *in camera*. In the end, 72 resolutions were passed at Québec, and it was agreed that they should be approved by the local legislatures without consulting voters. But in March 1865, the government of New Brunswick was forced to hold a general election. The incumbent ministers, who favoured Confederation, suffered a crushing defeat.

The federal union plan marked time, as it was impossible to federate Nova Scotia and the Province of Canada without including New Brunswick. But there was still hope, as the cabinet formed in New Brunswick after the March 1865 election consisted of men whose only affinity with each other was their opposition to the Québec resolutions; they disagreed on most other political issues. Such a government would find it difficult to survive for long. In April 1866, after several cabinet members withdrew their support, the premier was forced to tender his government's resignation. Backed by the British and financed in part by politicians in the Province of Canada – and helped along by an attempted invasion by the Fenians, an Irish-American paramilitary group devoted to the liberation of Ireland – the Confederationist candidates won the subsequent election handily.

At the same time, the legislatures of the other Maritime colonies took a stand on the federal plan: Newfoundland and Prince Edward Island were opposed; Nova Scotia was in favour. But in Nova Scotia, Joseph Howe mobilized public opinion in favour of putting the question to the people. The Fathers of Confederation, fearing defeat, turned a deaf ear. That fall, delegates from the colonies, with the exception of Newfoundland and Prince Edward Island, met in London to put the final touches on the plan. In October, John A. Macdonald, still haunted by the prospect of failure, warned one Canadian delegate already in England:

> It appears to us to be important that the Bill should not be finally settled until just before the meeting of the British Parliament. The measure must be carried *per saltum* [in one leap], and no echo of it must reverberate through the British provinces till it becomes law ... The Act once passed and beyond remedy the people would soon learn to be reconciled to it.
>
> *Ryerson 1973, 355*

The *British North America Act*, uniting New Brunswick, Nova Scotia and the Province of Canada in a single political entity, was given royal assent on March 31, 1867, and came into force the following July 1.

John A. Macdonald and the other Fathers of Confederation had won their wager: they had established a new constitution without going to the voters. Nova Scotia struck back, however; in the September 1867 general election, Nova Scotia sent only one federalist candidate to the House of Commons in Ottawa, while at the provincial level, all but two of the new members were anti-federalists. A few months later, delegates from the would-be secessionist province travelled to London to try to have the *British North America Act* repealed. Their efforts were in vain, but London did agree to have the federal government revise its policy on taxation, trade and fishing for Nova Scotia.

Having learned a valuable lesson, Prime Minister John A. Macdonald modified his strategy and decided not to impose Confederation on another colony without consulting the people through the polls. In the years that followed, his government negotiated agreements with Newfoundland, British Columbia and Prince Edward Island for their entry into the Confederation. Once agreements had been reached with the leadership in each colony, Macdonald insisted that an election be held. In 1869, the Newfoundland electorate voted overwhelmingly against joining Confederation. Two years later, British Columbia voters had their turn, but given the presence of a strong movement for amalgamation with the United States, the province's electorate had been selected carefully by establishing eligibility requirements to ensure sufficient numbers of pro-federation voters. The ploy succeeded, and British Columbia joined the union. Finally, in 1873, the people of Prince Edward Island agreed to join Confederation.

In short, only a small fraction of the voters in the founding colonies had been given an opportunity to decide their political future; the others were presented deliberately with a *fait accompli*. Since then, as subsequent events have shown, the relative influence of voters in Canadian parliamentary institutions has grown appreciably – to the point where today, politicians would not likely venture to act as the Fathers of Confederation did without consulting the electorate.

The Man in Charge
Édouard J. Langevin (1833–1916) was appointed Clerk of the Crown in Chancery on January 4, 1865, and held the office through Confederation until October 20, 1873. The Clerk was the federal official responsible for assembling and reporting election results to the House of Commons. The position was replaced by the Chief Electoral Officer of Canada in 1920.

CHAPTER 2

From a Privilege to a Right 1867–1919

At Confederation, the *British North America Act* stated that control of the federal franchise would remain a provincial matter until Parliament decided otherwise.

THE PROVINCES WERE still developing more or less independently, each with its own character rooted in its traditions, demography and geography. Inevitably, these differences were reflected in the provincial electoral laws that were to determine who could vote in federal elections for the first two decades of Confederation.

A Federal or a Provincial Matter

It was 1885 before Parliament took action. The Conservatives under Sir John A. Macdonald had been unable to reach consensus on a single set of voting eligibility criteria, while the Liberals, who supported a decentralized federation, wanted eligibility to remain under provincial control.

In 1885, however, Macdonald's government finally succeeded in having a law passed that gave Parliament control of the right to vote. The provinces regained control 13 years later, however, under a Liberal government led by Sir Wilfrid Laurier. As a result, in 10 of the 13 federal general elections held between 1867 and 1920, the electorate varied from province to province, with eligibility determined by provincial law.

The original colonies continued to adopt or adjust their electoral laws to meet their needs and circumstances. In addition, not long after Confederation, Canada experienced a huge territorial expansion that produced new provinces and territories, each of which adopted its own electoral legislation, adding further to interjurisdictional diversity in the electorate. Citizens of British Columbia and Manitoba took part in their first federal general election in 1872, Prince Edward Island in 1874, the Northwest Territories in 1887, Yukon in 1904, and Alberta and Saskatchewan in 1908.

Other factors, both regional and national, affected evolution of the right to vote during this period. These included demographic change, largely the result of massive immigration; urbanization and industrialization, and the accompanying enfranchisement of workers; and the emergence of a number of groups promoting women's suffrage. First Nations people were still effectively denied

After the Elections
Appearing first in the *Canadian Illustrated News* after the Quebec election of May 1, 1878, this cartoon by André Leroux of Montréal was adapted for the cover of the *News* after Sir John A. Macdonald's Liberal-Conservatives defeated Alexander Mackenzie's government later that year.

Yukon's First Wholly Elected Council, 1908
Voters elected two members for each of the territory's five constituencies (Klondyke, Bonanza, Whitehorse, North Dawson and South Dawson). George Black (*top row, second from right*) also represented Yukon in Parliament from 1921 to 1935 and 1940 to 1949. Martha Louise Black, his wife, held the seat while he was ill (1935–1940) and was Canada's second female member of Parliament.

access to the franchise either directly or indirectly at the regional and national levels.

Canada's geographic expansion in the second half of the nineteenth century was matched by population growth that continued into the early decades of the twentieth century. Between 1871 and 1921, the population more than doubled, from four million to more than eight and a half million. Growth was largely the result of immigration, although not all regions were equally affected. The Prairie provinces and, to a lesser degree, Ontario and Quebec attracted the largest numbers of immigrants. Over this period, the population of the Prairies shot up from 75,000 to almost two million.

Although many immigrants were of British origin, a large proportion were from Eastern Europe and Asia. In provinces where immigrants of neither British nor French origin formed a sizable minority, concerns about the electoral effects of the "ethnic factor" tended to be reflected in electoral legislation. Conversely, in provinces where the existing population did not feel threatened by the arrival of immigrants of different ethnic origins, ethnicity was not an important factor in voting eligibility.

Over the same period, urbanization and industrialization led to the emergence of workers' groups seeking to broaden the electorate. This is not surprising, given that in almost all provinces, the right to vote depended on property ownership or, in some cases, income level. These restrictions remained in force until the beginning of the twentieth century and persisted even longer in some provinces.

Property- or income-based qualifications effectively prevented large segments of the working population from voting. During the last quarter of the nineteenth century, most workers earned modest if not miserable incomes, and the vast majority were unlikely to own their own homes. In such conditions, any property-based qualification, no matter how minimal, was prohibitive. When the labour movement began to organize in the early 1870s, its representatives immediately demanded that the franchise be extended to lower-income groups. Some 20 years later, they demanded universal suffrage. It is difficult to know to what extent the demands of workers contributed to improving electoral legislation. One thing is certain: starting at the turn of the century, the provinces progressively eliminated property- and income-based restrictions on voting eligibility.

Questionable Election Practices

In the early days of Confederation, any individual who met the voting eligibility criteria could, in theory, exercise the right to vote. In fact, because of electoral practices common in those tumultuous times – when the value of a single vote was directly proportional to the limited number of electors – large numbers of electors were deprived of that right or obliged to cast their votes for a candidate selected by someone else.

Some of the rules in effect at that time did nothing to promote fair and equitable polling

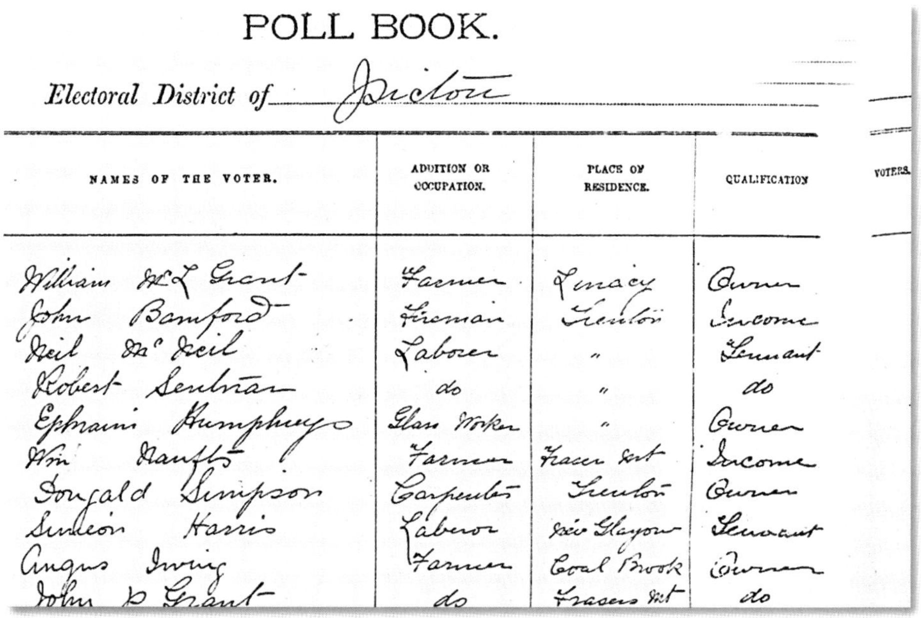

POLL BOOK.

Electoral District of Pictou

NAMES OF THE VOTER.	ADDITION OR OCCUPATION.	PLACE OF RESIDENCE.	QUALIFICATION	VOTERS.
William McL Grant	Farmer	Lenacy	Owner	
John Bamford	Fireman	Trenton	Income	
Neil McNeil	Laborer	"	Tenant	
Robert Sentrian	do	"	do	
Ephraim Humphreys	Glass Worker	"	Owner	
Wm Naufts	Farmer	Fraser Set	Income	
Donald Simpson	Carpenter	Trenton	Owner	
Simeon Harris	Laborer	New Glasgow	Tenant	
Angus Irving	Farmer	Coal Brook	Owner	
John D Grant	do	Frasers Mt	do	

The Changing Electorate

An expanded franchise brought new participants to politics. The Mechanics and Labourers of Ottawa presented a scroll (*left*) to Sir John A. Macdonald in 1878 "in sympathy with Liberal Conservative Rule." But a 1900 poll book for Pictou, Nova Scotia (*above*), shows that income was still a voting qualification. Researchers use poll books to link socio-economic, occupational and religious changes in the electorate to voting patterns. In 1985, renovators found this and dozens more poll books in the former home of Henri Lamothe, the federal official in charge of elections at the turn of the century; Lamothe had used them to insulate his attic.

practices. In all provinces but New Brunswick, which had adopted the secret ballot in 1855, electors voted orally, a polling method manifestly open to blackmail and intimidation.

Furthermore, in all provinces except Nova Scotia and Prince Edward Island, elections were held on different dates in different ridings. The system allowed the party in power to hold elections in a safe riding first, hoping in this way to influence the vote in constituencies less favourable to them. The system even enabled a candidate who lost in one riding to run again in another. In the 1867 general election, the Conservatives stretched the process over six weeks; in the next election (1872), they dragged it out for nearly three months. (See Appendix for dates and other information on these elections.)

After their 1874 victory, the Liberals passed two laws on election procedure. One measure withdrew the right to vote from a number of officials, including federally appointed judges and individuals who worked for candidates during an election (for example, as official agents, clerks or messengers), but this had little effect on the overall composition of the electorate. However, the measures also included several important mechanisms to help clean up questionable election practices: they introduced the secret ballot and stipulated that votes must be cast on the same day in all constituencies, they required candidates to disclose election expenses and they transferred hearings on contested election petitions from parliamentary committees to the courts. The reforms cleaned up the electoral process to some extent (for example, by reducing the use of violence to intimidate voters), but they did not eliminate all abuses.

Last of the Open Ballots, 1872
Sketches from the *Canadian Illustrated News* depict one of the last open-ballot elections, this one in Hamilton, Ontario. On the left, a torchlight parade to drum up voters. In the centre, successful candidates greet their supporters outside the newspaper office. On the right, the crowd's reaction as each man declares his vote from the hustings.

The figures on members who lost their seats because of fraud or corrupt electoral practices indicate the extent of the problem. Between 1867 and 1873, when petitions protesting the outcome of an election were presented to a committee of the House of Commons, just one of 45 contested elections was invalidated. When the courts began to look impartially at claims following adoption of the Liberal reforms, the number of voided elections soared. Between 1874 and 1878, 49 of the 65 contested elections submitted to the courts were voided, forcing nearly one third of the members of the House of Commons to resign. The rigorous approach of the courts appeared to lower the incidence of fraud, at least temporarily. Between 1878 and 1887, some 25 members were unseated following contested elections. Corruption flared up again, however, between 1887 and 1896, with some 60 members losing their seats after court challenges. By the end of the century, the number of members convicted of election fraud or corrupt

Elections cannot be carried without money. Under an open system of voting, you can readily ascertain whether the voter has deceived you. Under vote by ballot, an elector may take your money and vote as he likes without detection.

– John H. Cameron, MP
House of Commons *Debates*
April 21, 1874

practices began to decline again – not because of any improvement in election practices, but because of the political parties' increasing use of "saw-offs" – friendly agreements to withdraw equal numbers of contested election petitions before appealing to the courts.

Fraudulent practices took many and varied forms. One of the most common was to purchase votes through "treating" (the purchase of food and drink) or compensation. In addition to cash payment for votes, candidates or their agents might hand out alcohol, pork, flour and other foodstuffs. Personation – the illegal practice of voting in the place of another elector – also occurred on a large scale, especially in urban ridings where population mobility was much more prevalent.

Another practice was "importing" voters from the United States for election day – ferrying in Canadians who had moved to the United States. On March 6, 1891, a Quebec newspaper reported the arrival of two Grand Trunk Railway trains carrying some 2,000 textile workers from the United States who were returning home to vote. (Hamelin et al., 108) A decade later in Ontario, the Lake Superior Corporation (later the Algoma Steel Company) used a tugboat to bring in workers from Sault Sainte-Marie, Michigan, to vote in the place of absent or deceased miners.

Soon after adoption of Macdonald's *Electoral Franchise Act* in 1885, falsification of electoral lists became a common practice. Before that date, the lists, drawn up by municipal employees, had given rise to few complaints. Beginning in 1885, however, the lists were drawn up by persons appointed by the party in power. The name or profession of an elector was often changed, with the result that the person in question was not allowed to vote when he arrived at the polling station. At the same time, many individuals became "legally qualified" to vote when false names were added to the lists and the names of persons who had died or moved away were not deleted. To make matters worse, the lists were not updated regularly.

The 1891 election provides an excellent example of the combined effects of falsification of lists and lack of regular updating. In Ontario alone, comparison of the electoral lists updated in 1889 and census data for the year of the election reveals the existence of more than 34,000 "floaters" – persons who had died or moved out of the province. Moreover, because the 1891 election was held on the basis of lists revised two years earlier, tens of thousands of new electors were disenfranchised. In the country as a whole, according to contemporary accounts, at least 50,000 and possibly more than 100,000 electors were deprived of the right to vote

Campaign Literature, 1872

Malcolm Cameron (1808–1896) used the latest technology to produce this colour lithograph supporting his electoral bid, but voters chose another candidate. Cameron founded the *Bathurst Courier* at Perth, Upper Canada, in 1833 and was Queen's Printer for Canada from 1863 to 1869. His printing experience may have introduced him to colour lithography, which was not used widely until later in the century.

Nominations, 1871-Style
Sketch of the nominations in Montreal Centre for the Quebec provincial election held in 1871. The name of the artist is not known.

in that election because the electoral lists had not been updated or, in some cases, had been falsified.

Intimidation was another method used to influence election results. The Catholic clergy, for example, openly supported the Conservative party in pastoral letters and statements from the pulpit. Some parish priests even threatened their parishioners with the fires of hell if they voted Liberal. Although the effects of such intimidation were felt mainly in Quebec, where some elections were even voided because of the "undue influence" of the clergy, it was also a factor in the Maritimes, Ontario and Manitoba – until Rome and the courts reined in these tendencies around the turn of the century.

Intimidation by employers, though undoubtedly less widespread than the influence of the clergy, was nonetheless a factor. Employers threatened to reduce the wages of, or even fire, those who did not vote for the "right" candidate. The March 10, 1896, edition of *La Patrie* published the text of a notice posted on the wall of a Montréal manufacturing concern:

> We feel it is only fair to notify employees that, in case of a change in government [Conservative], we will be unable to guarantee the wages you are now being paid; neither will we be able to guarantee work of any kind to all the employees employed by us at this time.
>
> *Hamelin et al., 109, translation*

To the range of questionable election practices already described must be added the inappropriate use of public funds for election purposes, illegal election expenses, falsification of ballots and dishonesty, or even incompetence, among election personnel. In 1891, a returning officer in the Algoma riding said that he could distinguish between male and female "Indians" only on the basis of their clothing. Organizers for the Conservative candidate seized the opportunity: the men voted first, then lent their clothing to the women so they could vote.

The Electoral Mosaic, 1867–1885

From 1867 to 1885, five federal general elections were held, with the electorate varying from province to province under the provincial electoral laws then in force. In all provinces, there were three basic conditions for becoming an elector: being male, having reached the age of 21 and being a British subject by birth or naturalization. The other conditions varied according to the electoral law of each province. Tables 2.1 and 2.2 give an overview of the diversity of conditions in effect.

Table 2.1

Property and Income Qualifications: Minimum Conditions Required to Vote in Federal Elections, 1867–1885

Province	Value of real property, whether occupied by owners or tenants				Amount of annual rent		Annual income
	Owner or co-owner[1]		Tenant, co-tenant or occupant[1]		Tenant, co-tenant or occupant[1]		
	Urban area	Rural area	Urban area	Rural area	Urban area	Rural area	
Nova Scotia[2]	$150		$150		–		–
Quebec	$300	$200	–		$30	$20	–
Ontario[3]	$200	$100	$200	$100	–		$250 (urban residents)
Manitoba[4]	$100		$200		$20		–
New Brunswick[5]	$100[6]		–		–		$400
Prince Edward Island	Those under 60 years of age had to make an annual contribution of four days' work to maintain and build highways or the equivalent in cash; those over age 60 had to own real estate that generated a minimum annual income of $8.						
British Columbia[7]	No property or income qualifications.						

Notes:

1. The amounts indicated apply to each individual elector, including co-owners and co-tenants (e.g. for two co-tenants, the minimum value of the dwelling would be twice the amount stated in the table).
2. In Nova Scotia, the right to vote was given to the sons of anyone qualified to vote, on condition that the total value of the father's (or mother's, if the father was deceased) property was sufficient to qualify him to vote and that the son had not been absent from the family home for more than four months during the year preceding an election. Individuals whose total real and/or personal property was valued at at least $300 were also qualified to vote.
3. In Ontario, the right to vote was generally given to all residents whose names were included on a property assessment roll. An elector whose name did not appear on a list had to be, for at least six months before an election, the owner or tenant of real property granted by the Crown whose value met the requirements of the property qualifications then in effect.
4. In Manitoba, the right to vote was also given to any occupant of a dwelling located on land from which it was possible to derive income of at least $20 per year. In all cases, the period of residency was at least three months before an election.
5. Personal and/or real property of a total value of $400 also entitled individuals to vote in New Brunswick.
6. Property owners only.
7. In British Columbia, all electors had to have lived in the province for at least 12 months and in the riding for at least two months before an election.

Except in British Columbia, the main restrictions on entitlement to vote were property- or income-based qualifications, which established four classes of citizens: those who owned real property of a minimum value, those who leased or occupied a property of a minimum value or paid an annual rent of a minimum value, those who owned personal property or a combination of personal and real property of a minimum combined value and those who earned a minimum annual income. As Table 2.1 shows, electors were far from being equal across the country on the basis of these criteria.

For property owners, the required value of real property varied by as much as $300 from one province to another. Conditions for tenants and for those who qualified on the basis of owning a combination of real and/or personal property also varied widely. Finally, two provinces linked the right to vote to a minimum annual income: in Ontario, the minimum was $250; in New Brunswick, it was $400.

Three provinces – Ontario, Manitoba and British Columbia – imposed racial restrictions. Before Confederation, just one of the colonies had decreed that "Indians" could not vote. Nova

Table 2.2

Categories of Citizens Ineligible to Vote, 1867–1885

Nova Scotia	1. Any person who, during the 15 days preceding the election, was remunerated by the government as an employee of one of the following: • post office • customs • lighthouses • Crown land office • public works • mines • railroads • department of revenue 2. Any person in need who received social assistance or assistance in any amount from a charitable organization during the year preceding the election.
Quebec	1. Any person remunerated by the government as an employee of one of the following: • post office (cities and towns) • customs • Crown land office or holder of one of the following positions: • judge of the superior court, court of Queen's bench, vice-admiralty court, sessions court or municipal court • district magistrate • secretary, undersecretary or clerk of the Crown • sheriff or assistant sheriff • officer or member of a provincial or municipal police force 2. Any person who collected federal or provincial duties, including excise duties, in the name of Her Majesty.
Ontario	1. Any person of Indian origin or partly Indian blood, not enfranchised, who resided on a reserve located in a riding where no electoral list existed and who benefited from amounts paid, in the form of annuities, interest or other funds, to the tribe or band of which the person was a member. 2. Any person who, during the 15 days preceding the election, was remunerated by the government as an employee of one of the following: • post office (cities and towns) • customs • Crown land office or holder of one of the following positions: • judge • chancellor and vice-chancellor of the province • Crown clerk or assistant clerk • registrar general • prosecutor in a county court • sheriff or assistant sheriff 3. Any person collecting excise duties on behalf of Her Majesty. 4. Any person acting as returning officer or election clerk (deputy returning officers and poll clerks retained the right to vote). 5. Any person working in any capacity for a candidate before or during an election. 6. Any stipendiary magistrate (i.e. paid by an individual).
Manitoba	1. Any person of Indian origin who received an annuity from the Crown. 2. Any person holding one of the following positions: • judge of the court of Queen's bench, a county court or a municipal court • Crown clerk • registrar general • clerk of a county court • sheriff or assistant sheriff
British Columbia	1. Any person of Indian origin. 2. Any immigrant of Chinese origin. 3. Any person holding one of the following positions: • employee of the customs department • employee of the federal government responsible for collecting excise duties • judge of the Supreme Court or a county court • stipendiary magistrate • police constable or police officer 4. Any employee of the federal government paid an annual salary (except postal employees). 5. Any employee of the provincial government paid an annual salary. 6. Any teacher paid by the government of the province. 7. Any person previously found guilty of treason, serious crimes or other offences, unless he had been pardoned or served his sentence.

Scotia explicitly excluded Indians from the electorate in 1854 when it abolished property-based qualifications; when the province re-established these qualifications in 1863, it repealed the exclusion clause. In practice, in Nova Scotia as elsewhere, Indian persons were not entitled to vote because, under federal law, virtually none of them held property as individuals.

Soon after Confederation, Ontario decreed that, in places where no electoral lists existed, only "enfranchised Indians" – persons who had renounced their Indian status – could vote. If they wanted to exercise their right to vote, they could not be "residing among the Indians" or benefiting from amounts paid to a tribe or band in the form of annuities, interest or other funds. In ridings where electoral lists were drawn up, enfranchised Indians who did not reside among the Indians were eligible to vote, even if they received a portion of an amount paid to a tribe or band. In practice, however, this measure affected few people. In Ontario at that time, the number of enfranchised Indians could be counted on the fingers of one hand. Between 1867 and 1920, in all of Canada, a mere 250 Indian persons were enfranchised. We have no record of others who might have been covered by the terms of the legislation and could therefore have voted; their numbers were certainly not legion.

In Manitoba, Indians who received a benefit from the Crown were not entitled to vote. In British Columbia, neither Indian persons nor residents of Chinese descent could vote. Although there were very few immigrants of Asian origin in British Columbia at that time, Indian peoples accounted for more than half the province's population.

At the same time, all provinces except New Brunswick and Prince Edward Island denied the vote to certain government employees. Here, too, there was considerable inconsistency among the provinces. In Nova Scotia, for example, postal employees did not have the vote; in British Columbia and Manitoba, they did; in Quebec and Ontario, only rural postmasters were eligible to vote.

Amendments to provincial election laws between 1867 and 1885 did little to increase the number of electors, except in Ontario, where property requirements were reduced significantly, and in Nova Scotia, where the voting privileges of property owners were extended to tenants. At the same time, Nova Scotia, Quebec, Ontario and Manitoba extended the right to vote to co-owners and co-tenants of property assessed at a value that, if divided among the co-owners or co-tenants, fulfilled the property qualifications in effect for each individual. Considering the economic conditions of the period, this measure probably affected only a small number of individuals.

Macdonald Centralizes the Franchise

On July 27, 1885, Conservative Prime Minister Sir John A. Macdonald wrote to his friend Charles Tupper, "On the twentieth we closed the most harassing and disagreeable session I have ever witnessed in forty years." But he went on to add, "I consider the passage of the Franchise Bill the greatest triumph of my life." (Stewart, 3)

Why was Macdonald – who had won many other significant victories in his 40-year political career – so pleased with the bill? An ardent centralist, Macdonald had little use for provincial governments; if it had been up to him, they might have been abolished at Confederation. In the years preceding his franchise bill, the struggle between

Macdonald's Admission, 1873
The caption below this cartoon, published on September 26, 1873, quoted *The Mail* of the same date: "We in Canada seem to have lost all idea of justice, honor and integrity." Macdonald's support in the House of Commons declined after revelations that he had accepted campaign donations from Sir Hugh Allan, with whom he was negotiating government railway contracts. His government resigned on November 6.

the dominion and the provinces had intensified. Ontario, led by Oliver Mowat's Liberals, had won battles with the federal government on provincial boundaries and alcohol licensing. There seemed to be the risk of a snowball effect: in Nova Scotia, also led by a Liberal government, withdrawal from Confederation was touted as a real possibility. In this context, Macdonald could no longer allow the provinces to control the entitlement to vote in federal elections.

He tabled a bill giving full control of the franchise to the federal government. The bill led to unprecedented debate in the House of Commons. Between April 16 and July 6, 1885, members engaged in heated discussion of every facet of the legislation, often late into the night. The government finally had to concede a number of amendments. The result was an extremely complex elections act that, instead of producing a uniform Canadian electorate, diversified the electorate even more.

At a time when Ontario was preparing to expand access to the vote, Macdonald contrived to keep the property-based qualification. Along with most members of his party, he had a profound aversion to universal suffrage, which he considered one of the greatest evils that could befall a country. Perhaps convinced that most women were conservative, Macdonald suggested giving the vote to widows and spinsters who owned property. He backed down, however, in the face of objections from some of his own members, and the suspicion remains that Macdonald had inserted the clause as a sacrificial lamb, never intending that it survive final reading of the bill.

Macdonald's 1885 *Electoral Franchise Act* retained the three basic conditions common to all the provinces (being male, having reached the age of 21 and being a British subject by birth or naturalization). The property-based qualification differed according to whether an individual lived in an urban or a rural riding. Furthermore, in urban areas, it varied according to whether an elector lived in a city or a town (a distinction based on population size). Table 2.3 summarizes the resulting franchise across the country.

For example, to be qualified to vote in a city, a man was required to own real property valued at $300 or more. The occupant in good faith of a property of the same value was also qualified

Table 2.3

Minimum Conditions Required to Vote in Federal Elections, 1885[1]

Category	Value of real property, whether occupied by owners or tenants		Amount of annual rent	Annual income
	Owner or co-owner[2]	Tenant, co-tenant or occupant[2]	Tenant or co-tenant[2]	
Urban area	$300 (cities)[3] $200 (towns)		$2/month or $20/year	$300
Rural area	$150[4]		$2/month or $20/year	$300

Notes:

1. Under the terms of the *Electoral Franchise Act* of 1885, voting qualifications were the same in all provinces except Prince Edward Island and British Columbia. In those two provinces, where no provincially established qualifications existed, anyone who had the right to vote at the time the 1885 act came into effect kept that right; those who reached the age of 21 after that date had to meet the same qualifications as those in the other provinces.
2. The right to vote was given to sons of owners and tenants, on condition that the minimum value of the father's (or mother's, if the father was deceased) dwelling was sufficient to qualify him for the vote and the son had resided in the family home for 12 months without being absent for more than four or six months (depending on whether they lived in an urban or a rural area). In rural areas, owners' sons could be absent for more than six months without losing the right to vote if the reason for absence was working as a sailor or fisherman or attending an educational institution in Canada.
3. A city was a town with a population exceeding a number established by law.
4. Fishermen who owned real property and fishing gear (boats, nets, fishing gear and tackle) of a total value of at least $150 were also qualified to vote.

to vote. Tenants who paid a monthly rent of at least $2 or an annual rent of at least $20 could also vote, as could persons whose annual income was at least $300. Sons of owners or widows of owners whose total property value, divided among them, was sufficient to confer the right to vote on each of them, were qualified to vote, on the condition that a son had lived with his mother or father for one year with no break longer than four months. Furthermore, all electors except property owners were subject to a one-year residency requirement.

Prince Edward Island and British Columbia, where there had been no property-based qualification, received special treatment. In both provinces, anyone who already had the right to vote when the 1885 act was passed continued to enjoy that right; however, those who reached the age of 21 after that date were subject to the same property or income qualifications as those in effect in the other provinces.

The property-based qualifications set by the *Electoral Franchise Act* clearly favoured rural residents over urban dwellers. Furthermore, the qualifications

... there is so little likelihood of detection, [and] the price paid for passing false votes is so tempting, that unless severe measures are employed, there will always be persons willing to undertake the business.

– Herbert Brown Ames
quoted in John English
The Decline of Politics, 1977

were set higher than they had been before in most provinces. The act did give the vote to new classes of persons, on certain conditions, including fishermen, property owners' sons and farmers' sons (although they already had the vote in British Columbia and Prince Edward Island). At the same time, however, the act made it more difficult for small property owners and some tenants to obtain the right to vote.

The Last Hurrah, 1891
The name of the artist responsible for this familiar campaign poster – appealing to voters' fondness for the dominion's first prime minister – has not survived the years.

Comparing tables 2.1 and 2.3 shows that property owners saw the most significant increase in voting qualifications. In New Brunswick and Manitoba, the required value of property tripled for cities and doubled for towns; in rural areas, it rose by 33 percent. In Nova Scotia, it doubled for cities and climbed by 33 percent for towns, but remained the same in rural areas. In Ontario, the property qualification rose by 33 percent for both rural and urban areas. In Quebec, it remained unchanged for urban areas and fell by 25 percent for rural areas.

The situation with regard to tenants is more difficult to pin down. In the provincial laws that had previously applied, eligibility to vote was related to the value of leased property rather than the annual rent paid, making comparisons difficult. Under the 1885 act, at least some tenants became new members of the electorate. In New Brunswick, where no tenant had had the vote, the new law enfranchised those who paid the minimum required rent. In Manitoba and rural Quebec, the annual rent requirement was unchanged; in Quebec cities, it dropped by one third. Elsewhere, it can be assumed that the new law affected tenants adversely to the extent that the required value of leased property rose significantly.

Because we do not know the number of citizens in each category, it is impossible to arrive at an accurate figure for the electorate as a whole. It can be assumed, however, that the new electoral law reduced the overall size of the electorate. Residents of two provinces – British Columbia and Prince Edward Island, where universal male suffrage had almost been achieved – were clear losers. In these provinces, those who already had the right to vote kept it. But others reaching voting age were subject to the property-based requirements, which inevitably reduced the relative size of the electorate. The citizens of two other provinces were clear losers as a result of the changes: Ontario, because it was the most urbanized province and the legislation favoured rural residents, and Nova Scotia. These two provinces, both with Liberal governments in power, were precisely the provinces that had caused the biggest headaches for the Conservative government in Ottawa in the matter of the division of powers. In just one province – Quebec, a Conservative stronghold since 1867 – did the size of the electorate appear to have increased.

The 1885 act was more lenient than most of the previous provincial acts in terms of the right to vote of judges and some classes of government employees. Only the chief justice and justices of the Supreme Court of Canada and the chief justices and magistrates of provincial superior courts were prohibited from voting. Furthermore, some election officials (returning officers, poll clerks and revisers) were allowed to vote, but only in a riding other than the one where they worked. This rule also applied to all individuals who worked for a candidate in any capacity before or during an election.

The new election law retained existing racial restrictions and even disenfranchised some Indians in Quebec and the Maritimes. Persons of "Mongolian and Chinese race" were expressly deprived of the right to vote. According to John A. Macdonald, persons of Chinese origin ought not to have a vote because they had "no British instincts or British feelings or aspirations." (Roy, 152) Furthermore, the Indians of Manitoba, British Columbia, Keewatin and the Northwest Territories had no vote, and those living on reserves elsewhere in Canada were required to own and occupy a piece of land that had been improved to a minimum value of $150.

Macdonald was pleased, not only with recovering control of the franchise but also with ensuring that, from then on, the electoral lists would be drawn up by revisers appointed by the governor general in council, that is, by the government in power. These lists were the keystone of the electoral system. If an elector's name was missing from the list, he could not exercise his right to vote. Macdonald himself, on the advice of his supporters, appointed the revisers. Over the years, he established a complex countrywide network of his own appointees, which he controlled completely and effectively.

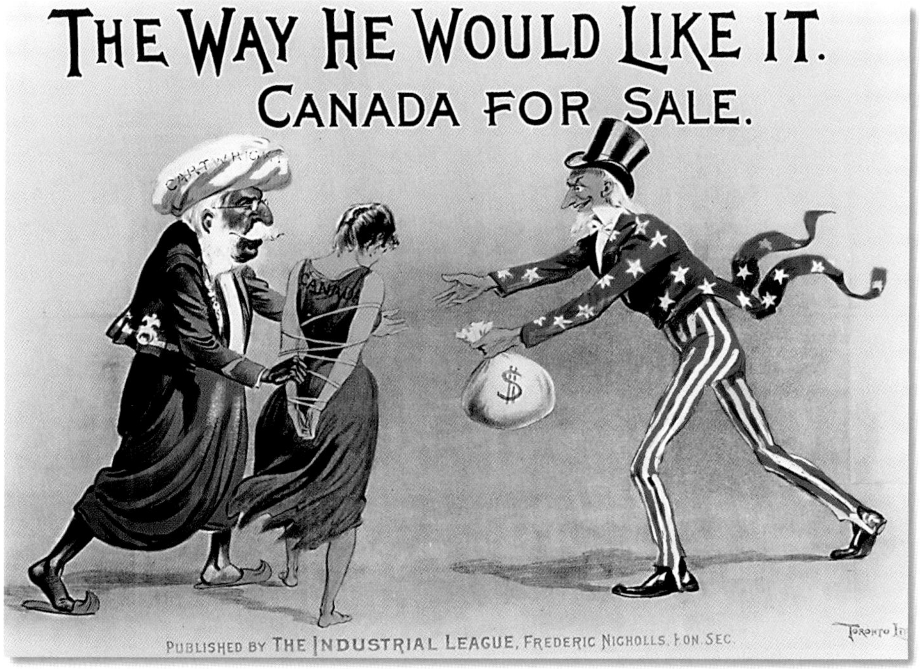

Perennial Issue?
Macdonald's Conservatives tried to persuade voters that a policy of reciprocity – one of the planks in the 1891 election platform of the Liberal party – amounted to selling Canada to the United States. The Conservatives were successful, but Sir John A. Macdonald died three months after winning the election.

Laurier Decentralizes the Franchise

For the Liberals, the 1885 election legislation was a bitter pill to swallow. They had only to wait for the right moment to change track. Macdonald died in June of 1891. Without him at the helm, the Conservatives soon foundered, and the Liberals under Wilfrid Laurier took power in 1896. When Charles Fitzpatrick, the solicitor general, tabled a proposed new electoral law in the House of Commons, he said that, since 1885, preparation of the electoral lists had cost the public coffers more than $1,141,000, an enormous amount for that time.

The new act, which took effect on June 13, 1898, was designed to correct the situation by giving the provinces responsibility for drawing up electoral lists and, once again, control of the right to vote in federal elections. The situation had regressed to pre-1885, including significant inequality among electors in different provinces.

To mitigate these disparities, the new federal law specified that the provinces were not empowered to disqualify voters. More specifically, the provinces were prohibited from excluding a citizen, otherwise qualified to vote, from exercising the right to vote on the grounds that he practised a particular profession or carried on a particular occupation, worked for the federal government or a provincial government, or belonged to any class of persons. As a result, citizens of Chinese or Japanese descent living in British Columbia obtained the right to vote in federal elections (even though they were excluded from provincial elections), as did federal and provincial government employees in Nova Scotia, Prince Edward Island, Quebec, Ontario and Manitoba.

The situation with regard to "Indians" was less clear-cut. At first glance, the wording of the act seems to suggest that Indians were also excluded from disqualification by provinces. There were indications, however, that in the minds of the legislators, Indians did not belong to "any class of persons." Until that time, the Liberals had always appeared reluctant to give Indians the right to vote. At its 1893 convention, the party made a formal statement condemning any measure of this kind. Later, the federal government refused Indian persons the right to vote in the Northwest Territories and Yukon, both of which were under direct federal control. It is therefore highly probable that the provisions disqualifying Indians from voting in provincial elections applied to federal elections as well.

In 1898, most provinces already applied significant restrictions on Indians' right to vote. No Indian was allowed to vote in British Columbia or New Brunswick. In Manitoba, the right to vote was reserved for Indian persons who received no benefit from the Crown and had received no such

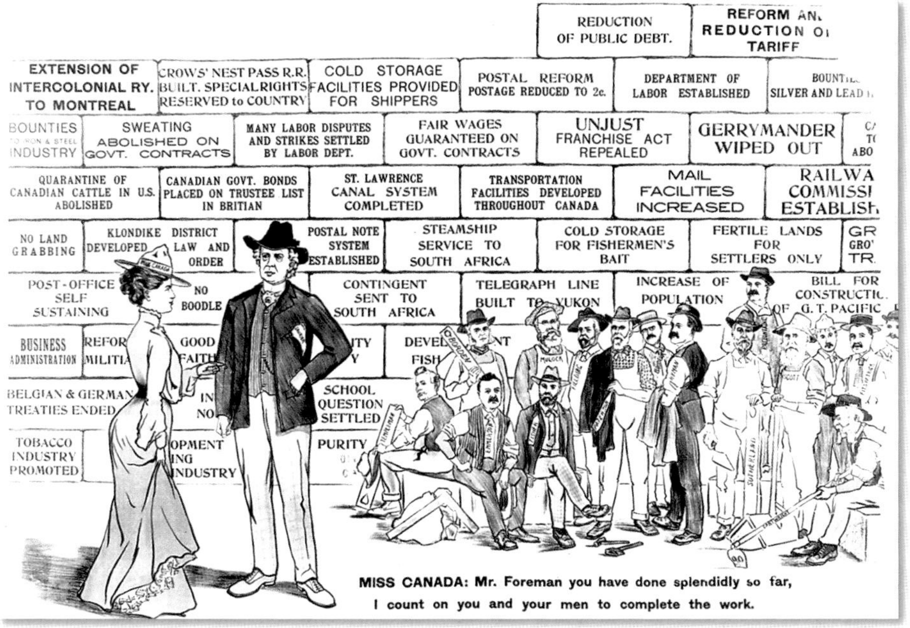

Running on Their Record, 1904
The Liberals appealed to voters with a wall of achievement – built of bricks that included "Unjust Franchise Act Repealed" and "Gerrymander Wiped Out." (The Liberals also took credit for "Increase of Population" and "Tobacco Industry Promoted.") Says Miss Canada (*left*) to Wilfrid Laurier, "Mr. Foreman you have done splendidly so far, I count on you and your men to complete the work."

benefit during the three years preceding an election. In Ontario, the right was given only to enfranchised Indians or Indians living outside a reserve, on condition that the latter own real property assessed at $200 or more in a city or town or $100 or more in a village or township. This last condition was even more discriminatory because Ontario had abolished all property-based qualifications for non-Aboriginal electors 10 years earlier.

The situation did not improve in the years that followed. In 1915, Quebec withdrew the voting rights of Indians living on reserves, and by July 1919, Indians living on reserves anywhere in the country were no longer entitled to vote in federal by-elections.

The Liberals' 1898 election law excluded other groups as well, among them previously excluded federally appointed judges. Furthermore, three classes of individuals already disqualified from voting in Manitoba, Ontario and New Brunswick – prison inmates, and residents of lunatic asylums and charitable institutions receiving assistance from a municipality or the government – were now disenfranchised throughout the country. In addition, persons who, before or during an election, were hired by another person and remunerated in any way for working as an agent, clerk, solicitor or legal counsel were also disenfranchised. Electors found guilty of election fraud lost the right to vote for seven years. Finally, returning officers and poll clerks were prohibited from voting in the riding in which they performed their duties. All these exclusions remained in force until at least 1920.

The 1898 act specified that the conditions that qualified a person to vote in a federal election were the same as those that qualified the individual to vote in provincial elections in his province of residence. This principle was more restrictive than it appeared at first glance. Because statutory disqualification was no longer permitted, the provinces were left with some half-dozen factors that they could use to control the right to vote: age, gender, citizenship, length of residence and property-based requirements. The first three qualifications were already common to all provinces. From Atlantic to Pacific, only males age 21 or over who were born or naturalized British subjects were qualified to vote. Residency requirements, which varied from province to province, might apply to the province as a whole, to the electoral district or to both.

The required length of residence in the province was six months in British Columbia and 12 months everywhere else; for particular ridings, the provisions ranged from one month to 12 months. Ontario, the most urbanized of the provinces, added a specific provision with regard to cities and towns, where changes of domicile were extremely common. The residency requirement was 12 months in the province, three months in the town in question and one month in the riding. These provisions tightened restrictions on urban electors, who often moved in pursuit of work, without penalizing them too harshly.

Before 1920, only two provinces changed their residency requirements. In 1907, New Brunswick halved it, from 12 months to six. The same year, Ontario relaxed its 12-month residency requirement to include residence anywhere in the country, though the additional residency requirements for urban areas remained in place. A few provinces accepted the fact that some individuals (loggers,

After the Elections, Part 2
The 1878 Quebec provincial election resulted in numerous cartoon depictions of the vanquished and the victor (see also page 40). This one, from the *Canadian Illustrated News*, is by J. W. Bengough of Montréal.

Family Connections, 1902
This card urged electors to nominate and vote for T. F. Wallace but did not achieve its goal: Wallace lost the 1902 by-election. Wallace was likely a relative of Nathaniel Clarke Wallace, member of Parliament for West York from 1878 until his death in 1901, and of Thomas George Wallace, who held the seat from 1908 to 1921.

TO THE FREE AND INDEPENDENT ELECTORS

OF

West York

Your Vote and Influence are respectfully requested for the election of

T. F.

WALLACE

As Member for the House of Commons.

Nomination Day, 8th January. Polling Day, 15th January, 1902.

Central Committee Room 28 Yonge St. Arcade, Toronto. God Save the King sailors, students) were occasionally or temporarily absent from their usual residence to carry on their occupation or attend an educational establishment. In 1900, the federal government decreed that military personnel and war correspondents did not lose the right to vote because of absence for reasons of active duty. The measure, which affected all provinces, was adopted to accommodate Canadians serving in the Boer War in South Africa. When the war ended two years later, the privilege granted to Canadian servicemen remained in place.

Before adoption of the 1898 act, property-based qualifications were the main curb on expansion of the electorate. At that time, this restriction still existed in only four provinces: Prince Edward Island, New Brunswick, Nova Scotia and Quebec.

In Prince Edward Island, property-based qualifications affected only persons 60 years of age or over, who were required to own real property assessed at at least $100 or generating a minimum annual income of $6. In 1902, the province achieved universal male suffrage when it abolished the requirement. To qualify to vote in New Brunswick, it was necessary to own real property assessed at $100 or more, or real property and personal property with a combined value of $400. Persons earning an annual income of $400 were also qualified to vote. This threshold was very high; at the turn of the century, a textile worker, for example, earned an average of $240 per year. New Brunswick abolished property- and income-based qualifications in 1916.

In Nova Scotia, the situation had remained unchanged since 1885. To be qualified to vote in the province in 1898, it was still necessary to own, rent or occupy property assessed at $150 or more. Furthermore, an individual who owned personal property and leased or occupied property whose

The lists used in [the 1908 federal] election were provincial lists which had been compiled two or more years earlier, and contained the names of many dead and absent persons. However, by a custom regarded as common and ordinary, the votes of the dead and absent were not lost but were made good use of by both contesting parties.

– Charles G. ("Chubby") Power
A Party Politician, 1966

value, added to that of the personal property, totalled $300, was qualified to vote. Co-owners, co-tenants, sons of men qualified to vote and widows who owned, occupied or leased property with a value sufficient to confer the right to vote could vote under the same conditions as those that existed before 1885. The province later qualified as electors persons earning an annual income of at least $250 and fishermen who owned real property, boats, nets and fishing tackle with a combined value of $150 or more. Property- and income-based qualifications were eventually eliminated in the province in 1920.

In Quebec, where urbanization was in full swing, the property-based qualifications in force in 1898 still favoured residents of rural areas. In urban areas, owners or occupants in good faith of premises assessed at $300 could vote; in rural areas, the minimum required value was just $200. A similar disparity existed between tenants in urban areas, where the minimum annual rent was $30, and tenants in rural areas, where it was $20. Persons receiving a minimum annual income of $300 were also qualified to vote. Fishermen could vote if

Broadcasting the News, 1911
In the days before mass media, broadcasting an election proclamation required a bucket and paste brush (Lambton County, Ontario, photographer unknown).

they owned boats, nets, seines and fishing tackle worth a total of $150 or more. Furthermore, retired farmers and property owners (referred to as life annuitants) could also vote if their annuity – in cash or in kind – was $100 or more. Teachers were exempt from any property-based requirement. In 1912, Quebec substantially reduced financial qualifications, a measure that gave the right to vote to the great majority of men in the province.

The 1898 federal legislation certainly expanded the Canadian electorate. To what extent? Because censuses from that era are relatively unreliable, it is impossible to say. One thing is certain: when the legislation was adopted, most provinces, including Ontario (the province with the largest population), had already introduced universal male suffrage. In these provinces, therefore, universal male suffrage also applied to federal elections. This was a significant step forward from Macdonald's 1885 legislation, which not only maintained the principle of property- or income-based qualifications but even raised the eligibility threshold in most areas of the country. Laurier's 1898 law broadened the electorate even further by prohibiting provincial disqualification based on race or socio-professional characteristics. Nonetheless, two provinces – British Columbia and Manitoba – tried to find ways to get around the federal legislation.

In 1901, British Columbia decreed that no one could vote if he was unable to read the provincial election legislation, which was written in English. Naturally, this measure was hostile to the enfranchisement of citizens of Chinese or Japanese origin. The following year, Manitoba adopted a similar strategy: no one was qualified to vote who could not read the Manitoba elections act in English, French, German, Icelandic or a Scandinavian language;

this effectively prohibited many immigrants of Polish, Ukrainian and Russian origin from voting in federal elections. The record does not show whether the federal government intervened to counteract these efforts at disenfranchisement.

Borden's Strategic Measures

After Canada declared war on Germany in August 1914, the country fell victim to a wave of collective hysteria. The commander of the naval yard at Esquimalt, British Columbia, was so fearful of a German invasion that he succumbed to nervous collapse. Fear of spies gave rise to general mistrust of new Canadians, especially those from Germany or Austria-Hungary. At that time, immigrants from these countries accounted for about 5 percent of the population of Canada. In October 1914, the federal government interned foreign nationals identified by government officials as a potential danger to the country. More than 8,500 individuals were sent to closely guarded internment camps.

Three years later, the war dragged on, and volunteers for military service had begun to fall short of requirements. By April 1917, a total of 424,526 Canadians had volunteered to serve overseas. In April, the number of volunteers was only 5,530; in May, it was up slightly at 6,407. But Canadian losses at the front were high: in April alone, 3,600 Canadians were killed and 7,000 wounded at the battle of Vimy Ridge. The Conservative prime minister, Robert Laird Borden, travelled to England and returned shaken by the experience. To him, there was only one solution: in June, he tabled a military service bill authorizing the government to conscript any male person between the ages of 18 and 60.

Borden's government was already in serious trouble, however, and an election was imminent. Could the conscription issue defeat them at the polls? This was what was predicted in the West, where the largely immigrant population already sympathized strongly with Laurier's Liberals, and the conscription issue seemed to be strengthening the trend. Across the country, union leaders got ready to do battle with conscriptionists. In Ontario, the rural population opposed conscription, and francophone Quebec rejected conscription spontaneously and massively.

Borden and his government, who saw their situation as increasingly desperate, attempted to modify the composition of the electorate by changing the electoral law. Borden confided to his diary, "Our first duty is to win at any cost the coming election so that we may continue to do our part in winning the war and that Canada be not disgraced." On September 20, 1917, Parliament adopted not one, but two election acts, though Borden had to use closure to push them through.

The first, the *Military Voters Act*, was designed to increase the number of electors potentially favourable to the government in power. As its title suggests, the law defined a military voter as any British subject, male or female, who was an active or retired member of the Canadian Armed Forces, including Indian persons and persons under 21 years of age, independent of any residency requirement, as well as any British subject ordinarily resident in Canada who was on active duty in Europe in the Canadian, British or any other allied army. (Thus, some 2,000 military nurses – the "Bluebirds" – became the first Canadian women to get the vote; see next section.) Furthermore, military voters could assign their vote to any riding in which they

Making the Vote Accessible, 1916–1917

Special arrangements for electors unable to vote because of disability, occupation or assignment abroad were introduced gradually to improve access to the vote: the postal ballot (1915), advance polling (1920), proxy voting (1970) and level access at polling stations (1992, although level access had generally been available since 1988 as a result of Elections Canada's administrative requirements). These photos show soldiers voting overseas in the federal election of December 1917 (*above*) and the British Columbia election of September 1916 (*right*).

had previously been domiciled, failing which their vote could be assigned by the party of the military voter's choice to the riding where it would be most useful. Finally, the act contained a short section that appeared innocuous but was extremely significant: several hundred thousand votes from overseas would be counted only 31 days after an election in Canada.

The second law, the *War-time Elections Act*, had a dual purpose: to increase the number of electors favourable to the government in power and decrease the number of electors unfavourable to it. The law conferred the right to vote on the spouses, widows, mothers, sisters and daughters of any persons, male or female, living or dead, who were serving or had served in the Canadian forces, provided they met the age, nationality and residency requirements for electors in their respective provinces or Yukon. It also conferred the right to vote on those who did not own property in accordance with prevailing provincial law but had a son or grandson in the army. (This provision affected only Quebec and Nova Scotia, as the other provinces had already abolished property- and income-based qualifications.)

The act also disenfranchised conscientious objectors. This affected Mennonites and Doukhobors, even though the federal government had exempted them officially from military service, the former in 1873 and the latter in 1898. Individuals born in an enemy country who became naturalized British subjects after March 31, 1902, were also disenfranchised, with the exception of those born in France, Italy or Denmark and who arrived in Canada before the date on which their country of origin was annexed by Germany or Austria. Also included were British subjects naturalized after March 31, 1902, whose mother tongue was that of an enemy country, whether or not the individual's country of origin was an ally of Great Britain. The same rule applied to persons found guilty of an offence under the *Military Service Act*, 1917. Overall, new Canadians living on the Prairies were the most seriously affected by the *War-time Elections Act*, with tens of thousands being disenfranchised.

Finally, the legislation of September 20, 1917, stripped the provinces of the responsibility for drawing up electoral lists and gave the task to enumerators appointed by the federal government – in other words, by the Conservatives as the party in power. The president of the Canadian Suffrage Association remarked that the act would have been more honest if it had simply disenfranchised everyone who failed to promise to vote for the Conservatives! All Borden had to do now was call an election.

But the race was not yet won. One week after the two laws were passed, an informant with sources in government circles reported to Laurier that the Conservatives, fearing defeat, were preparing to mobilize English-Canadian opinion against French Canada. Who among Borden's inner circle had devised the strategy? One thing was certain: Borden did not reject it. In the next few months, the English-language press painted a picture of Quebec as a province that was as big a threat to Canada as Germany was to the world.

Cases of election fraud soared during the subsequent election campaign. A soldier suspected of intending to vote Liberal was threatened with being sent immediately to the front. Telegrams and letters

Women and the Vote, 1867–1900

1867 *British North America Act* entrenches women's exclusion from the vote.

1873 Female property owners in British Columbia are first "Canadian" women to gain right to vote in municipal elections.

1876 First women's suffrage group set up in Toronto under the guise of a literary society.

1885 Sir John A. Macdonald introduces, then withdraws, an elections act amendment giving women the vote.

1894 Women's Enfranchisement Association of New Brunswick formed.

Manitoba Equal Suffrage Club founded.

House of Commons votes down a petition for women's suffrage presented by the Women's Christian Temperance Union.

1900 By this date, most women property owners have the vote in municipal elections.

The Suffragette Movement
Nellie McClung was a women's rights activist who helped found the Manitoba Political Equality League in 1912 and led the movement to enfranchise Canadian women. In 1916, Manitoba women were the first to gain the right to vote in provincial elections. Women gained the right to vote in 1918 at the federal level.

from the federal cabinet even specified the number of floaters to be entered on the electoral lists to assure election of a given candidate in a given riding. An officer who feared investigation of the irregularities was told that anyone who failed to hold their tongue would be buried in France within six months. Efforts to exercise "undue influence" on the election resurfaced on a scale previously unheard of. The Sunday preceding the election, in three out of four Protestant churches across the country, pastors and ministers exhorted the people to look on voting for the government in power as a sacred duty, failing which Canada would be disgraced.

The election was held on December 17, 1917. As specified in the *Military Voters Act*, the votes of civilian electors were counted before those of military voters. The military vote was more than 90 percent for Borden. The Conservatives won at least 14 additional seats by redistributing the military vote to ridings where opposition candidates had a slight lead. Borden won the election. But was Canada less "disgraced"? The proposition is doubtful at best. A few days before Canadians went to the polls, Sir Wilfrid Laurier remarked to Sir Allen Aylesworth, one of his oldest friends, "The racial chasm which is now opening at our feet may perhaps not be overcome for many generations."

Women and the Vote

The Bluebirds who voted at the 1917 federal election may have been the first Canadian women to do so with the official sanction of the electoral law behind them, but they were not the first North American women to vote.

At Confederation, all the original colonies had statutory provisions excluding women from voting,* and these were entrenched in section 41 of the *British North America Act*:

> Until the Parliament of Canada otherwise provides, all laws in force in the several Provinces of the Union … shall … apply to elections of Members to serve in the House of Commons … [and] every male British Subject, aged Twenty-one Years or upwards, being a householder, shall have a vote.

The colonies (except for Lower Canada) inherited England's common law tradition, under which women had not exercised the franchise for centuries; this was the result of convention, not statute law. (Garner, 156) In the colonies, the convention seems to have been less influential.

Only New Brunswick explicitly prohibited voting by women before 1800. There, the council banned women from voting in the colony's inaugural election, held in 1785, but the assembly later failed to include the ban in the colony's first electoral law, passed in 1791.

In Upper and Lower Canada, the *Constitutional Act* of 1791 was silent on the issue of women voting, extending the franchise to "persons" who owned property of a certain value. Not being subject to the common law, women in Lower Canada turned out to vote at several locations. Madame Rosalie Papineau, mother of Louis-Joseph, voted for her son at the 1809 election, declaring her choice "a good and faithful subject." The women accompanying her also voted. By the 1820 election the practice had spread, and voting by women was recorded in Bedford County and Trois-Rivières, where a local citizen wrote later that two members

*Only Upper Canada never used statute law to close the franchise to women. But after the union of Lower and Upper Canada, the Province of Canada disenfranchised women in 1849.

had been elected by the "men and women of Trois-Rivières, for here women vote just as men do, without discrimination." In Trois-Rivières, one man was even disenfranchised because he had placed his property in his wife's name. On election day, "the unhappy man appeared at the polling place, only to find himself doubly humiliated by being refused the franchise and then sent to get his wife to the polls because she was the qualified voter in that family." (Cleverdon, 215)

In Upper Canada, the common law tradition seems to have prevailed, since we have no written accounts of women voting or records of election-related complaints involving voting by women.

Two recorded incidents in Nova Scotia make it clear that women voted there. The first involved a disputed election in Amherst Township and the second an 1840 election in Annapolis County, where the Tories made great efforts to use women's votes to save the riding from a Reform landslide and the Reformers countered by transporting their own female supporters to the polls. The Tory effort was in vain. The Reform women did not even have to vote – they turned out at the polls in such large numbers that the Tory women returned home without voting. (Garner, 156)

The 1840 *Act of Union*, uniting Upper and Lower Canada in the Province of Canada, contained no prohibition on voting by women, and neither colony had a law against it. At least seven women voted in the 1844 election in Canada West – the first recorded occurrence of a violation of the common law practice. This came to light as a result of a protest by the defeated Reform candidate that seven women had voted for his Tory opponent. When they returned to power in 1849, the Reformers used the occasion of a general consolidation of

A Woman Votes in Lower Canada, 1827

A handwritten record of names, qualifications, challenges and votes for the election of July 25, 1827, shows that Agnes Wilson's vote (left-hand column, fourth name from the bottom) was not challenged. Women in Lower Canada were not bound by the common law convention barring women from the polls.

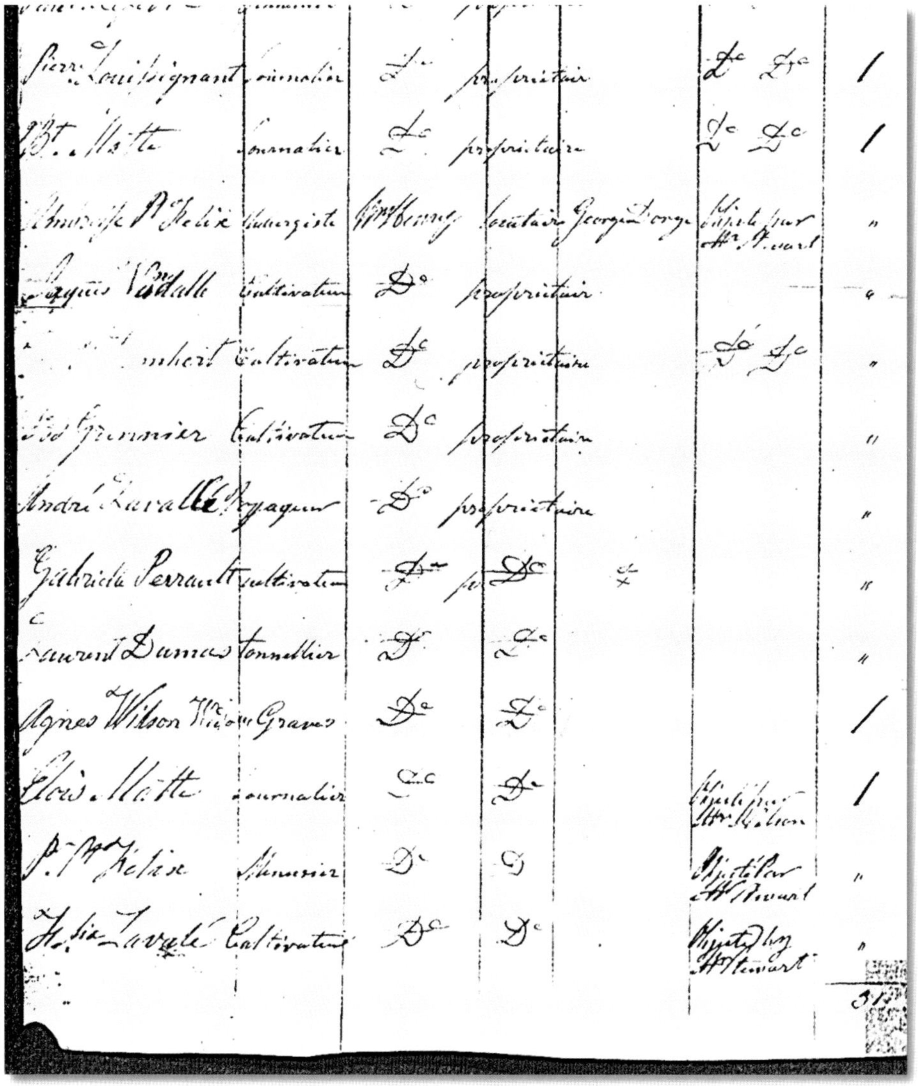

Women and the Vote, 1912–1921

1912 Manitoba Political Equality League founded in Winnipeg.
Montreal Suffrage Association formed.

1914 Flora Macdonald Denison, suffragette journalist and president of the Canadian Suffrage Association, publishes *War and Women*.

1915 Edmonton, February. Nellie McClung, heading one of the largest delegations to the Alberta legislature ever assembled, presents a petition demanding the vote for women.
Winnipeg, December. Suffragists present a 45,000-name petition to Premier Tobias C. Norris.

1916 January. Manitoba women are the first in Canada to win the right to vote in provincial elections.
March. Saskatchewan women get the vote.
April. The suffrage movement triumphs in Alberta.

1917 February. Ontario women get the vote but still cannot sit in the legislature.
April. British Columbia women get the vote.
Serving members of the armed forces (including women) get the federal franchise through *Military Voters Act.*
Female relatives of soldiers at the front get the vote through *War-time Elections Act.*

1918 May 24. Royal assent given to bill giving women the right to vote in federal elections. Eligibility: age 21 or older, not alien-born and meet property requirements in provinces where they exist.

1919 Electoral law amended – women can now stand for federal office.

1920 Federal electoral law amended; changes include universal female (and male) suffrage regardless of provincial law.

1921 First federal election at which women vote under universal franchise.

electoral laws to insert a clause excluding women from the vote.

The female franchise had already begun to contract in 1834, when Lower Canada's legislative assembly attached a clause restricting voting by women to an act dealing with controverted elections.* The pretext was that polling stations had become too dangerous for women. (Violence during the 1832 election had resulted in three deaths.) The 1830s also saw the rise of ultramontanism, a conservative clergy-led movement that was to affect many aspects of Quebec society. The *Imperial Reform Act* of 1832, which restricted the franchise in the United Kingdom to men, may also have been influential.

Another force was at work as well: cultural politics. Events in Bedford County demonstrated that restriction of the franchise may have been less the result of hostility to women voting than of language and cultural tensions. In Bedford, the defeated candidate complained to the assembly that his opponent had been elected in part by the votes of 22 married women – in other words, husbands and wives had exercised the right to vote on the basis of the same pieces of property.

The assembly responded by resolving that the women's votes had been illegal, but the resolution seems to have been prompted by the fact that the women's votes had elected an English-speaking candidate at the expense of the French-speaking incumbent. This impression is reinforced by an incident eight years later, when petitioners contested the election of Andrew Stuart after an English-speaking returning officer in Québec refused to accept one woman's vote for Stuart's French-speaking opponent. (Garner, 157)

Whatever the source of the restriction, and regardless of the fact that the 1834 law was later struck down, increasing social conservatism seems to have done its work, and women in Lower Canada appear to have ceased voting in significant numbers. (Hamel, 227)

*The law was later overturned by colonial authorities in London for reasons unrelated to women's right to vote.

Table 2.4
Women's Democratic Rights

	Right to Vote	Right to Be a Candidate
British Columbia	1917	1917
Alberta	1916	1916
Saskatchewan	1916	1916
Manitoba	1916	1916
Ontario	1917	1919
Quebec	1940	1940
New Brunswick	1919	1934
Prince Edward Island	1922	1922
Nova Scotia	1918	1918
Newfoundland	1925	1925
Canada	**1918**	**1919**

Between that time and Confederation, the female franchise was eroded further. Women were disenfranchised by law in Prince Edward Island in 1836, in New Brunswick in 1843 and in Nova Scotia in 1851. Two years earlier, in 1849, the Reform government of the Province of Canada had gained legislative approval for a law prohibiting women from voting: "May it be proclaimed and decreed that no woman shall have the right to vote at any election, be it for a county or riding, or for any of the aforesaid towns and cities." This ended years of confusion about the validity of the female franchise in the Canadas.

This was the situation at Confederation: women of property in the various colonies had enjoyed the franchise (or at least had not faced legal restrictions), then lost it over a period of years and for a variety of reasons. With provincial law governing the federal franchise at Confederation, this exclusion was entrenched in the new dominion's constitution.

Within a decade after Confederation, however, a women's suffrage movement had begun in almost all the former colonies. The exception was Quebec, where extreme conservatism still held sway in social, political and religious matters. Elsewhere in Canada, the push for women's suffrage had taken hold by the 1870s. The first suffrage societies were established by women seeking social, economic and political equality with men. Many were professionals, often pioneers in fields such as medicine, who had encountered discrimination first-hand. (Bacchi, 433) This decade saw the founding of the Toronto Women's Literary Club by Dr. Emily Stowe, Canada's first female doctor, in 1876. The club was in fact a screen for suffrage activity and thus was the country's first suffragist organization, changing its name in 1883 to the Toronto Women's Suffrage Association.

But soon the suffrage movement took on a different cast, attracting men and women of Protestant, Anglo-Saxon origins, most of whom belonged to the educated urban middle class – professionals,

[Women's suffrage] is a matter of evolution and evolution is only a working out of God's laws. For this reason we must not attempt to hurry it on.

– James P. Whitney
The Daily Mail and Empire
March 21, 1911

Sisters in the Struggle, 1916
British suffragette Emmeline Pankhurst was photographed in 1916 at the Edmonton home of Nellie McClung. Mrs. McClung is in the centre, wearing a striped dress; Mrs. Pankhurst is to her left. Also in the group was Emily Murphy (author, suffragist and later a judge), one of the five complainants in the 1929 "Persons Case," in which the British Privy Council determined once and for all that Canadian women were indeed "persons" and therefore eligible for appointment to the Senate.

clergymen, a few reform-minded businessmen and their wives. (Bacchi, 433) These suffragists had a broad social reform agenda, one that embraced workplace safety, public health, child labour, prohibition of the production and sale of alcohol, prostitution, the "Canadianization" of immigrants as well as votes for women. The Women's Christian Temperance Union (WCTU), for example, became a force in the suffrage movement, convinced that if women had the vote, temperance would be assured.*

Similarly, social reformers intent on combatting the evils of industrialization and the urbanization that accompanied it – abuse of alcohol, prostitution, venereal disease, neglect of children – joined the suffrage movement with the goal of bolstering the social order with what might now be called "family values." Giving women the vote would double the family's representation and extend maternal influence into the political sphere.

In Quebec, the picture was different. As the suffrage movement elsewhere in Canada was taking its first steps, Quebec moved to prohibit women voting in municipal elections and amend the Civil Code to make women legally "incapable" – of owning property, of inheriting an estate and certainly of voting. Advocates of women's rights in that province therefore focused more on gaining legal reforms and equality of opportunity in education than on the vote. It was not until the 1930s that the focus shifted to women's suffrage. Also apparent was the influence of conservative clergy and nationalists who objected to the Anglo-Saxon origins of the suffrage movement.

In the 1880s, debate about women's suffrage became linked with provincial autonomy issues. Until 1885, under the terms of the *British North America Act*, the provinces determined who was eligible to vote in federal elections. Prime Minister John A. Macdonald changed that with the *Electoral Franchise Act* of 1885, whose passage he considered the greatest triumph of his life. (Stewart, 3) In consolidating control of the franchise at the federal level, Macdonald even included a clause giving propertied widows and single women the vote, though he later withdrew it: apparently it had been a sacrificial lamb never intended to remain in the final version of the law. Sir Wilfrid Laurier's Liberal government returned the federal franchise to provincial control with a new electoral law in 1898. The focus of suffragist activity therefore

*The first Canadian section of the WCTU was founded by Laetitia Youmans at Picton, Ontario, in 1874.

shifted to provincial governments and legislatures, where it remained for the next two decades.

By the end of the nineteenth century, then, the women's suffrage movement was well underway, with organizations active in the Western provinces, Ontario and the Maritimes. The municipal franchise was extended gradually; by 1900, most women property owners across the country could vote in municipal elections.

In addition, bills to give women the vote had been introduced in New Brunswick, Nova Scotia, Ontario and British Columbia, though none was successful. Between 1885 and 1893, and again between 1905 and 1916, a bill introduced annually in the Ontario legislature to give women the vote provoked laughter and derision. Bills were also introduced in the New Brunswick legislature in 1886, 1894, 1895, 1897, 1899 and 1909; all were defeated (some by only a narrow margin) or allowed to die on the Order Paper. Women presenting petitions at the time the 1909 bill was introduced were greeted by insults, whistles and jeers from MLAs in the corridors, who asked the sergeant-at-arms to ring the division bells until the women left the building.

To counter these attitudes, Canada's suffragists relied on petitions to provincial governments – sometimes containing as many as 100,000 names; on lecture tours and speaking engagements; on meetings with politicians; and on public meetings and events, such as mock parliaments (see box *right*). The confrontational tactics adopted by British and American campaigners for women's suffrage had no counterpart in Canada.

The suffragists were well organized, willing to buck social convention and skilful at enlisting the help of influential organizations, particularly in the West, where they gained the support of the United Farmers' Association of Alberta and the Grain Growers Association. As has been the case with other social issues in Canada, the Western provinces led the way in enfranchising women. Manitoba was the first, extending the provincial franchise to women in January 1916. Saskatchewan and Alberta followed suit in March and April respectively. The next year, 1917, Ontario women got the vote in February and British Columbia women in April. Also that year, Louise McKinney of Alberta, a temperance and women's rights advocate, became the first woman elected to a Canadian legislature.

This broadening of the provincial franchise, coupled with extension of the franchise to propertied women in municipal elections, created pressure for change at the federal level. But the immediate impetus was political, and women's first access to the federal franchise was almost accidental. On the eve of the 1917 general election, the government of Sir Robert Borden faced a complicated situation: women in all provinces from British Columbia to Ontario had the vote by virtue of provincial electoral law; women living east of the Ontario/Quebec border did not. Without some standardization of the franchise, ridings in Ontario and the West would have twice as many electors as those in Quebec and the Maritimes.

The temporary solution that presented itself had less to do with women's rights than with the pressing political issue facing Borden's government: conscription. As described earlier in this chapter, Parliament extended the franchise through two new laws in a transparent effort to expand the pro-conscription ranks. The *Military Voters Act*, intended to enfranchise soldiers under the age of 21,

Votes for Men!

Women's suffrage groups often staged public events to advocate their cause. One event, sponsored by the Manitoba Political Equality League in Winnipeg in January 1914, featured a play with women in the role of legislators listening to a group of men petitioning for the vote. Nellie McClung, in the role of provincial premier, rejected the idea, declaring that "Man is made for something higher and better than voting. Men were made to support families. What is a home without a bank account!" McClung, who had had many run-ins with Premier Rodmond Roblin on the women's suffrage issue, mimicked him so well that the audience often roared with laughter.

Chronicle of Canada, 557

Bluebirds at the Ballot Box, 1917
Given the time difference between Europe and Canada, these Canadian military nurses (the "Bluebirds"), photographed at a polling station set up at a Canadian field hospital in France in December 1917, probably voted before women in Canada. If so, they were among the first Canadian women to vote in a dominion election.

inadvertently benefited women as well, so that the Bluebirds – military nurses serving in the war effort – became the first Canadian women to exercise the right to vote in a federal election.

The second law, the *War-time Elections Act*, gave the vote to close female relatives of people serving in the armed forces (swelling the electoral lists by some 500,000 names), but it also effectively withdrew the vote from women who would otherwise have had it by virtue of provincial law but did not have a relative in the armed forces. This situation would not be tolerated for long.

The following year, Borden's re-elected government moved to correct the situation, introducing a bill to provide for universal female suffrage on March 21, 1918. Again, the bill was not universally welcomed. Declared MP Jean-Joseph Denis, "I say that the Holy Scripture, theology, ancient philosophy, Christian philosophy, history, anatomy, physiology, political economy, and feminine psychology all seem to indicate that the place of women in this world is not amid the strife of the political arena, but in her home." (*Debates* April 11, 1918; 643) Facing strong opposition, Borden compromised by stipulating in the bill that women electors would have to meet the same requirements as men – for example, property requirements where they existed. The compromise worked, and the *Act to confer the Electoral Franchise upon Women* received royal assent on May 24, 1918. A 1919 law gave women the right to be candidates in federal elections.

Women's suffrage was "in the tide," as Nellie McClung told Alberta legislators in 1915. The "fresh wind" of change felt by McClung in Alberta had now swept across the land. Nova Scotia women gained the provincial franchise in 1918.

Legislation in 1920 provided universal access to the vote without reference to property ownership or other exclusionary requirements – age and citizenship remained the only criteria. Provincial control of the federal franchise was now a thing of the past. The general election of 1921 was the first open to all Canadians, men and women, over the age of 21. Agnes Macphail, the first female member of Parliament, won a seat at that election.

CHAPTER 3

Modernization 1920–1981

We have seen how the right to vote expanded gradually until the First World War and then how the electorate doubled when women gained the franchise. By 1920, nearly all adults had the right to vote, although many individuals were still disenfranchised by administrative arrangements, and some groups were disqualified on racial, religious or economic grounds.

AT THE BEGINNING of the period covered in this chapter, few special measures were in place to protect the right to vote by facilitating voting or encouraging those who had the franchise to exercise it. The conventional procedure for casting a ballot – an elector appearing in person at the polling station on the day set for the election – was the only available option. Citizens were presumed to:

- be present in the riding on the appointed day
- have the time needed to get to a polling station and vote
- hold employment that did not interfere with voting
- have no characteristics – such as a disability or language difficulty – that might pose an obstacle to voting

Sixty years later, these assumptions were recognized as faulty and no longer held sway in electoral law and administration.

This chapter traces how the law and election administration have been shaped and reshaped to accommodate the broad diversity that characterizes the Canadian electorate. Legislative and administrative innovations made voting more accessible and convenient, modernized the election machinery, and removed racial and religious disqualifications.

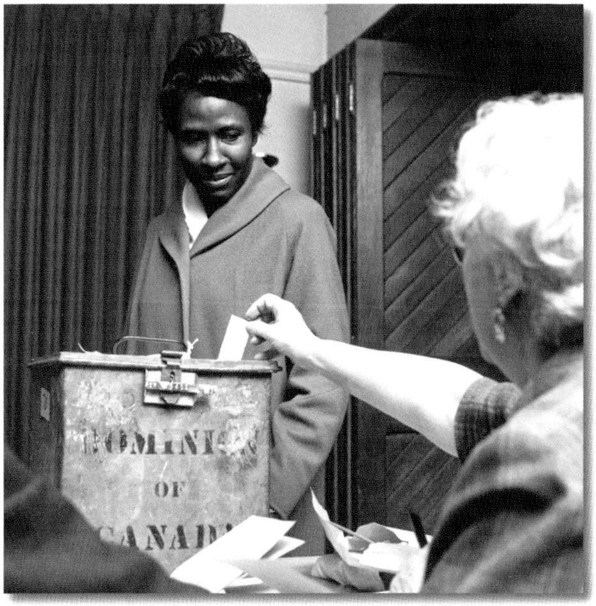

Decision Day, 1963

A Toronto voter looks on as the deputy returning officer places her ballot in the ballot box. It was not until 30 years later, when the electoral law was amended (Bill C-114, passed in 1993 and discussed in Chapter 4), that voters were entitled to place their own ballots in the ballot box.

Prophetic Pronouncement, 1917
Sir Wilfrid Laurier feared the effects of the 1917 election on French-English relations and opposed some of the changes in electoral law that preceded it, but he remained opposition leader after the votes were counted. This image is from a postcard used in Laurier's 1911 campaign.

A New Era Dawns, 1920
Despite criticism of his 1917 election tactics, Sir Robert Laird Borden, prime minister from 1911 to 1920, is credited with ushering in the modern era of electoral law with passage of the *Dominion Elections Act*, predecessor of today's *Canada Elections Act*.

As we learned in Chapter 2, Sir Wilfrid Laurier feared the *War-time Elections Act* would open an abyss that might not close for generations. Laurier was referring to a clash between Canadians of French and British origin, but in the years immediately after the First World War, it seemed that the hysteria of 1917 might extend to other groups as well. Anti-German sentiments, for example, did not fade entirely with the end of the war. During social disturbances such as the Winnipeg General Strike of 1919, anti-alien feelings were widely expressed. In the 1920s, hostility to racial and religious minorities swept across North America, and these feelings intensified until 1945. One way this hostility was expressed was in exclusionary electoral laws.

But not all developments in the franchise were negative. The *War-time Elections Act* governed just one election, that of 1917, being replaced under Borden's Conservative government by the *Dominion Elections Act* in 1920.* The act established the post of Chief Electoral Officer and isolated the incumbent from immediate political pressures by specifying appointment by a resolution of the House of Commons, not by the government of the day. Thus began the tradition of an independent, non-partisan agency administering the electoral process – in fact, the first such agency in the world.

The new act gave the Chief Electoral Officer the status of a deputy minister and the tenure of a superior court judge, which at that time was for life. During debate on the act, there was opposition to lifetime tenure. J. A. Currie, the MP for Simcoe North, said, "You are only setting up a form of Prussianism when you are appointing officers for life." Other MPs also questioned the value of the office. But many agreed with Norman Ward's assessment: "a most salutary reform." (Ward, 181)

The first Chief Electoral Officer, Oliver Mowat Biggar, presided over what could have been the most chaotic election in years. No fewer than 75,000 newly minted election officials were appointed to supervise a completely redesigned process serving an electorate that, including women, was more than double the number of those eligible to vote before 1917. Despite these innovations, Biggar recounted in his statutory report that the problems involved in the election process itself were comparatively small, given the large number of people involved.

An important job of the Chief Electoral Officer was, and still is, to prepare a report after each election. The report, required under the *Canada Elections Act*, gives the Chief Electoral Officer a regular opportunity to assess how the electoral law is working and to suggest reforms to Parliament. Many of these have concerned access to the vote – how to ensure that electors can exercise their franchise. This, too, has had positive effects on the electoral process, as Parliament has adopted and extended many such recommendations.

In his report after the 1921 election, for example, Colonel Biggar recounted the difficulties of

*The title was changed to the *Canada Elections Act* in 1951.

Chief Electoral Officers and Their Times

Just five people have held the position of Chief Electoral Officer since it was established in 1920.

Oliver Mowat Biggar (1920–1927), the first Chief Electoral Officer, oversaw the development of federal election administration under the new law. It was his task to implement a system that centralized financial and organizational aspects of federal elections for the first time. Under him, reforms were begun to improve the accuracy and completeness of federal voters lists and to make advance polling more widely accessible.

Jules Castonguay (1927–1949) launched the first attempt to establish a permanent list of electors. The last vestige of property qualification was eliminated during his tenure. He was responsible for introducing, in 1935, the short-lived innovation of sending a postcard telling each registered elector where to vote. Dropped in 1938, the postcard was reintroduced in 1982, when technological advances made the practice more cost-effective. During his term of office, a system was introduced that allowed Canadian military personnel serving overseas to vote.

Nelson Jules Castonguay (1949–1966) saw the end of religious discrimination in the law, extension of the franchise to all "registered Indians," and introduction of the *Electoral Boundaries Readjustment Act.* During his tenure, special arrangements were made for electors in sanatoriums, chronic care hospitals and homes for seniors. Voting by postal ballot became available to spouses of military personnel posted abroad, and the right to vote in advance polls was made available to everyone who would be away from home on election day.

Jean-Marc Hamel (1966–1990) implemented many changes in election law and administration, including registration of political parties, establishment of an election financing regime controlled by the 1974 *Election Expenses Act* and the creation of the position of Commissioner of Election Expenses, which in 1977 became the Commissioner of Canada Elections. After 1982, Mr. Hamel oversaw the execution of amendments arising from legal challenges to the *Canadian Charter of Rights and Freedoms.* During his term in office, the voting age was lowered from 21 to 18 years, and measures to increase the accessibility of the vote for electors with disabilities were put into place.

Jean-Pierre Kingsley (1990–) adopted a proactive role for his office by recommending and promoting key initiatives. While continuing the reforms needed to comply with the Charter, he ushered Elections Canada into the age of computerized election administration. Under his leadership, Elections Canada gained a new mandate to inform and educate voters, particularly those most likely to experience difficulties in exercising their democratic rights. Other achievements include the introduction of the 36-day election calendar, digitized electoral geography systems and products, and the establishment of the National Register of Electors. As well, the election financing regime was expanded to regulate third-party advertising and election financing of all political entities. With content ranging from election results to financial reports of political entities, the Elections Canada Web site was developed as a tool for public information. During Mr. Kingsley's tenure, Elections Canada participated in many significant international development missions aimed at the promotion of democratic electoral processes through co-operation, capacity building and mutually beneficial relationships. Following his recommendations to Parliament, the *Canada Elections Act* was amended in 2006 to authorize the Chief Electoral Officer to appoint returning officers.

Oliver Mowat Biggar

Jules Castonguay

Nelson Jules Castonguay

Jean-Marc Hamel

Jean-Pierre Kingsley

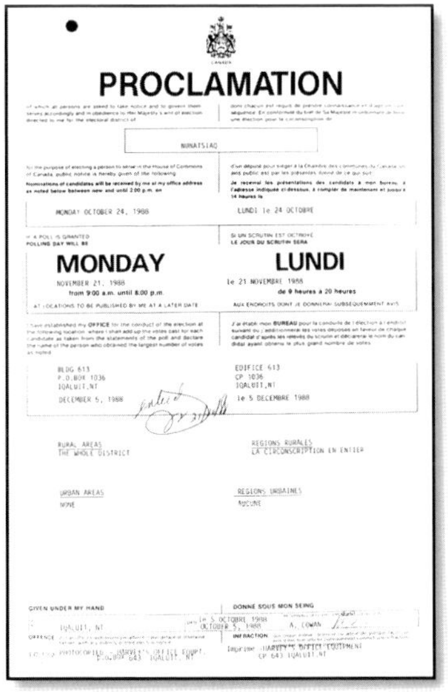

Never on Sunday

Since 1929, the law has specified that elections are to be held on a Monday unless that day is a federal or provincial holiday, in which case voters cast their ballots on Tuesday. Election proclamations have followed a similar format for the past 200 years (see also illustration, page 7). This 1988 proclamation is for Nunatsiaq, which was then Canada's largest riding in area (a distinction held since 1993 by Nunavut) and its smallest in population.

electors – particularly women – who had been left off voters lists. He suggested the appointment of more revision officers and advised making more advance polls available. Parliament responded by reducing the number of voters needed for setting up an advance poll from 50 to 15.

Similarly, after the 1925 election, Colonel Biggar pointed out that with the election being held on a Thursday, the advance voting provisions had been of little use to commercial travellers: they were already out on the road when the advance polls opened for the three days preceding the election. In 1929, the law was changed to establish Monday as election day.

The *Dominion Elections Act*

Parliament's overhaul of the electoral law in 1920 not only established the post of Chief Electoral Officer but also centralized the financial and logistical operations of federal election administration for the first time. It was a comprehensive revision of the election law, yet flaws remained in the system, some of which were not removed until the 1980s.

The most serious deficiencies were the continuing obstacles to voting for some female electors; exclusion from the franchise of specific groups for racial, religious or economic reasons; and administrative disenfranchisement of individual voters. In the last category were a number of small but irritating hindrances, many of which were cleared up by periodic electoral reform between 1920 and 1982.

Voters Lists

As was the case before 1920, the new law provided for elections to be conducted on the basis of lists of electors; in urban areas, the lists to be used were provincial lists compiled previously, but in rural areas, an enumeration would be conducted. These lists proved contentious, not only in their compilation, but also in what they contained and how they were published. The most serious problem – placing the names of eligible women on the electoral rolls – was solved by 1929, but methods of preparation, revision and publication continued to be debated and modified over the years.

The reason for the distinction between "rural" and "urban" polling divisions and the two different methods of compiling and revising voters lists was concern about the completeness and accuracy of existing voters lists in rural areas. This fear was borne out in the 1921 election, when lists from rural Ontario proved virtually useless.

The law, therefore, stipulated that in rural polls (places with a population of less than 1,000), lists were to be "open." People would be enumerated by specially appointed "registrars" in a door-to-door canvass. Voters missed by the enumeration could swear themselves in on election day, as long as another voter named on the list vouched for them.

But in urban polls, voters left off a provincial list had to apply to a revisions registrar – one was available in each constituency for 10 hours a day for six days. After this time, urban lists were "closed" until the next election. The argument used to justify this difference in treatment was that rural areas were harder to canvass, so election day swearing-in was needed to protect the franchise of rural voters. It was not until 1993, when Bill C-114 eliminated the distinction between urban and rural polling divisions, that urban voters had access to this provision.

The urban/rural distinction appears to have been a significant impediment to the exercise of the franchise for many electors. Some constituencies contained both rural and urban polls, and voters did not always know which type of poll they lived in – which meant that they might not take the steps necessary to have their names added to the list. In addition, to add to electors' confusion, a few months before the 1921 election, the definition of "rural" polls was changed. Now towns with a population of less than 2,500 were considered "rural." (This number was subsequently revised several times.)

But the most serious impact that became apparent in the 1921 election was that large numbers of women seemed to have been prevented from voting, despite the removal of legal restrictions in 1917–1918.

In Quebec, for example, women did not have the vote in provincial elections. (Indeed, Alexandre Taschereau asserted that they would never get it so long as he was premier – which he was until 1936.) As a result, women's names did not appear on provincial voters lists. In rural polls, women left off the lists could swear an oath on election day; in urban areas, they had to apply to a registrar within the specified period to have their names added to the list.

The results are apparent in the figures for elector registration. In Ontario, 99.7 percent of the population aged 21 or older was registered; the comparable figure in Quebec was 90.6 percent. The nine-point difference is the equivalent of 107,259 people. As there were 581,865 women aged 21 or over in Quebec in 1921, it seems likely that the vast majority of unregistered people were women, who were thus unable to exercise the federal franchise.

In 1929, the act was amended to abolish the use of provincial voters lists, making it much easier for Quebec women to be registered on federal voters lists, even though they did not gain the provincial franchise until 1940.

Exercising a New Right, 1921
It was women like these members of the Manitoba Political Equality League who were behind the successful struggle for women's suffrage. But at the 1921 general election, the first at which women could vote under the universal suffrage provisions of the *Dominion Elections Act*, some women learned that having the right to vote and exercising it were two different things. One of the difficulties was ensuring names were on voters lists.

These changes did not come without protest. The Conservative leader, Arthur Meighen, felt that allowing swearing-in on election day in towns of 2,500 could lead to fraud. Charles G. ("Chubby") Power, a Liberal member of Parliament, agreed, saying that some people might show their patriotism "through their willingness to vote more often than the law considers judicious." (*Debates* June 19, 1925; 4548) Despite these warnings, there appears to have been little such "patriotism" in the ensuing decades.

Beginning with the election of 1930 and until the 1990s, most federal elections were conducted using lists assembled by enumerators during the election period. For most of this period, urban enumerators worked in pairs; in rural areas, there was only one enumerator per poll. In urban areas, enumerators were appointed from lists of names

Privacy Matters
The location of polling stations was clearly posted for all to see during the 1963 general election. The same practice applied to voters lists until 1982, when concerns about privacy prompted its abandonment, to be replaced by a voter notification system based on postcards sent to everyone who had been enumerated. Since 1997, however, preliminary voters lists have been compiled from the National Register of Electors, following the 1996 amendment to the *Canada Elections Act*.

submitted to each returning officer by the parties of the candidates placing first and second in the electoral district in the previous election.

Once lists were compiled through enumeration, voters – particularly in urban polls – had to make sure that their names appeared if they wanted to be able to cast a ballot. A few copies of the pertinent list were posted in every polling division so that voters could check on the accuracy of the enumeration. In his 1926 report, Colonel Biggar stated that the lists had been drawn up in haste, that publicly posted lists were subject to damage by weather and vandals, and that many people felt they had been left off "on party grounds." Since revising officers were normally partisan appointees, simple mistakes were often attributed to bad faith. Biggar suggested that there should be wider access to the lists so people could check their accuracy more easily.

Jules Castonguay, the second Chief Electoral Officer, took up the issue again after the 1930 election, reporting that there was no easy way for voters to protect their right to vote by ensuring they were on the voters list. He suggested that every household receive a copy of the list for the relevant poll. This recommendation was adopted – eventually – after a different method was tried in 1934.

The Election "Telegram"

Despite steady improvement in electoral law, the "telegram," a form of electoral fraud well known in the nineteenth century, did not disappear until the middle of the twentieth century. Campaign organizers "sent a telegram" by giving a voter an illegally obtained ballot already marked in favour of the organizer's candidate. Inside the booth, the voter concealed the blank ballot received from the deputy returning officer, then emerged with the pre-marked ballot, which was placed in the ballot box. Presenting the blank ballot would garner a "reward" from the organizer, who would then mark the ballot and repeat the process with another voter. Since the reward was received only after the ballot was cast, a voter could swear with impunity before entering the booth that he had received neither money nor other inducements. This fraudulent practice was finally laid to rest with the introduction of administrative controls.

Too Young to Vote, 1942

The rules governing eligibility to vote in federal elections also apply to federal referendums. Here, the Rooney Club of Toronto uses a dog cart to promote a "Yes" vote in the plebiscite on conscription for overseas military service, held on April 27, 1942. The other national referendums were on prohibition (1898) and the Charlottetown Accord (1992). In 1992, Parliament adopted the *Referendum Act* to govern the conduct of consultative referendums on the constitution.

The Enumerator's Challenge, 1965
"But Rodney, are you sure the Geneva Convention requiring you to give only your name, address and social security number applies?" As this cartoon by *The Vancouver Sun*'s Len Norris suggests, the enumerator does not always get co-operation. With the advent of the National Register of Electors in the spring of 1997, enumeration is now a thing of the past.

The 1934 innovation was to send each registered elector a postcard showing where to vote. The Chief Electoral Officer's report described this as "quite onerous," because each card had to be addressed individually. The postcards were dropped after this election, and from the 1940 election until 1982 (when postcards were reintroduced), voters were sent a copy of the list showing the name, address and occupation of all voters in the relevant poll.

The government of R. B. Bennett also introduced a standing list of electors (a form of permanent voters list) in 1934. There was to be a final enumeration, and constituency registrars would revise the lists annually after that. All voters lists, both rural and urban, would be "closed" – anyone left off inadvertently would have to apply to be put on and could not vote until that was done.

One annual revision was undertaken, and the list was used for the election of 1935, but financial constraints prevented revision of the electoral register after that. The technology of the day was insufficient to overcome the logistical obstacles, so the effort was abandoned in 1938, and enumeration was restored as the method of compiling lists.

MPs who had experienced Bennett's electoral register system saw it as far too expensive and cumbersome, and even the Chief Electoral Officer, whose reports were normally circumspect, said that it was no improvement on the pre-election enumeration system. Jules Castonguay observed that the updated elections act had not worked effectively. Sending individually addressed postcards to notify electors was costly and time-consuming, he said. The government adopted Mr. Castonguay's suggestion of sending a poll list to each voter, and the idea of a permanent list did not resurface until the 1980s.

Access to the Vote

A significant innovation of the 1920 elections act was the provision for voting in advance of election day by specified groups of voters: commercial travellers, railwaymen and sailors could vote during the three days (excluding Sundays) preceding an election.

Although most people would consider advance voting a positive step, the provision was controversial from the first. A former minister of finance, W. S. Fielding, saw it as a waste of money; it was, he said, "like creating a steam engine to run a canoe" for a mere handful of voters. Fielding maintained that railwaymen and others should cast their votes by proxy. This would interfere with the secrecy of the ballot, he conceded, but most men, at least in his home province of Nova Scotia, made no secret of how they voted, so the loss of secrecy did not matter much. (*Debates* April 13, 1920; 1163)

This grudging attitude toward advance voting endured for decades. In 1934, it was extended to workers in "airships" (as aircraft were described in the law until 1960) and to fishermen – although MPs pointed out that fishermen were unlikely to be in port for the brief advance polling period if it occurred during fishing season.

The advance polls were available only to voters who expected to be absent from the riding on business on election day; they had to swear to this and obtain a certificate. It was thus no easy matter to vote at an advance poll, even if a voter was among the lucky few who qualified.

Another step that improved access to the vote was legislation increasing worker entitlement to time off for voting. The measure was first introduced in 1915, when employers were required to give their workers an hour off while the polls were open (in addition to their lunch hour). In 1920, this was increased to two hours.

During the interwar years, the only new group to obtain the vote consisted of people receiving public charitable support or care in municipal poorhouses (who had not been enumerated in the past because they lacked a "home" address). They received the franchise in 1929. On the whole, the two decades after the First World War were marked by modest but steady improvements in the conditions under which electors exercised the right to vote.

The Second World War and Its Aftermath

The next stage in the evolution of the franchise saw the lifting of racial and religious restrictions on voting, some of which had been in effect for many years. It was also a period of innovation in the accessibility of the vote, with legislative and administrative changes to facilitate voting and make it more convenient for electors.

The interval between the world wars saw the spread of antagonism toward minority groups in Canada. A degree of mistrust or suspicion of "aliens" had persisted since the First World War. As is common in periods of economic distress, this grew into hostility toward minorities during the Great Depression of the 1930s, exacerbating the social conflicts arising from competition for scarce jobs and societal resources. Finally, the crisis of the Second World War provoked further racial animosity, particularly toward Canadians of Japanese origin.

One result of these powerful social currents was the continued disqualification of particular groups on racial or religious grounds. Many ordinary Canadians seemed to accept these developments as a fact of life. To their credit, some MPs from all parties opposed racism and social injustice in

The Bearer, whose photograph and specimen of signature appear hereon, has been duly registered in compliance with the provisions of Order-in-Council P. C. 117.

Vancouver
(Date) March 12 1941.

JAPANESE NATIONAL

Issuing Officer
INSPECTOR R.C.M.P.

Japanese Canadians
In addition to being registered and interned during the Second World War, citizens of Japanese origin had been excluded from voting since British Columbia joined Confederation in 1871. This internment identification card, belonging to Sutekichi Miyagawa, was presented to the National Archives of Canada in 1975, along with a collection of related items.

impassioned speeches in the Commons. But in the pervasive climate of intolerance, especially in the 1930s, their voices did not prevail.

When the Second World War was over, Canadians seemed to realize that they had mistreated minority groups, and disenfranchisements of earlier years began to be reversed. By 1960, when all Status Indians were finally granted the unconditional right to vote, disqualifications on racial and religious grounds had been eliminated altogether. At the same time, legislative and administrative change was making it possible for more and more Canadians to exercise their right to vote in various ways.

Racial Exclusions

One of the significant exceptions to universal adult suffrage in the *Dominion Elections Act* of 1920 was a clause stating that people disenfranchised by a province "for reasons of race" would also be excluded from the federal franchise. In 1920, only one province – British Columbia – discriminated against large numbers of potential voters on the basis of race. British Columbia excluded people of Japanese and Chinese origin, as well as "Hindus" – a description applied to anyone from the Indian subcontinent who was not of Anglo-Saxon origin, regardless of whether their religious affiliation was Hindu, Muslim, Sikh or any other. Saskatchewan also disenfranchised people of Chinese origin, although the number of persons affected by the exclusion was much smaller than that in British Columbia.

British Columbia had a long history of such discrimination: when it entered Confederation, 61.7 percent of the province's population was of First Nations or Chinese origin, while people of British origin accounted for 29.6 percent of residents. Under successive provincial governments, measures excluding First Nations people and people of Asian ancestry from the franchise were extended as immigration increased toward the end of the nineteenth century.

The exclusion was challenged in the *Homma* case of 1900, but in 1903, the Judicial Committee of the Imperial Privy Council (at that time the ultimate court of appeal for Canada) upheld the prerogative of the British Columbia legislature to decide who could vote in provincial elections.

Denial of the franchise had far-reaching implications, because provincial law also required that pharmacists, lawyers, and provincial and municipal civil servants be registered on the voters lists. As a result, Canadians of Japanese and Chinese origin were barred from these professions and from contracting with local governments, which had the same requirement.

Even military service was not enough to qualify people of Asian ancestry for the vote. After the First World War, the British Columbia legislature decided, following much debate, not to give the vote to returning veterans of Japanese origin, much less to other Japanese Canadians. Some had voted in the 1917 federal election – under the terms of the *Military Voters Act*, provincial disqualification had not deprived them of the federal vote. In the debate on the 1920 elections act, however, Hugh Guthrie, the solicitor general of the day, made clear his objection to enfranchisement:

> So far as I know, citizenship in no country carries with it the right to vote. The right to vote is a conferred right in every case ... This Parliament says upon what terms men shall vote ... No Oriental, whether

he be Hindu, Japanese or Chinese, acquires the right to vote simply by the fact of citizenship ...

Debates *April 29, 1920; 1821*

Guthrie maintained that his government was not discriminating but merely recognizing "the provincial disqualification imposed by the law of any province by reason of race."

In 1936, a delegation of Japanese Canadians asked the House of Commons to extend the franchise to them. Prime Minister Mackenzie King said that he had been unaware that they wanted the franchise. A. W. Neill, MP for Comox–Alberni, an area with a significant Japanese Canadian population, said the request for the franchise was "sob stuff" and "claptrap." Another member for British Columbia, Thomas Reid, suggested that the whole affair was a plot to enable the Japanese government to plant spies in British Columbia. Needless to say, given such views, the franchise was not extended.

The war years and the bombing of Pearl Harbor brought expulsions and internment for Canadians of Japanese origin. In 1944, Parliament amended the *Dominion Elections Act* to deny the vote to the Japanese Canadians forced to leave British Columbia and relocate in provinces where they had not previously been disqualified from voting. Extending British Columbia's racially based disenfranchisement laws to the rest of Canada provoked considerable reaction from MPs representing other provinces.

The Co-operative Commonwealth Federation (CCF) member for Cape Breton South, Clarence Gillis, said:

While we know that the war with Japan is a serious matter and that many atrocities have been committed by the people of that country, there is no reason why we should try to duplicate the performances of that country.

Arthur Roebuck, the Liberal MP for Toronto–Trinity, said that he

... could not face the minority groups in my own city – the Ukrainians, the Poles, yes the Italians, and many others – if I allowed

Two Sides of the Question

Thomas Reid, an MP representing New Westminster, British Columbia, opposed extending the franchise to Canadians of Japanese origin in 1936. Clarence Gillis, member for Cape Breton South, Nova Scotia, opposed the government's plan to extend racial restrictions on the franchise in 1944. Reid's point of view prevailed in 1936. The objections of Gillis and some other MPs were ignored, and restrictions on citizens of Japanese origin were not lifted until 1948.

Thomas Reid

Clarence Gillis

this occasion to pass without making
myself absolutely clear before this House
and the country that, when it comes to
racial discrimination against anybody,
count me out.

Not all members were of like mind, however. A. W. Neill supported the disenfranchisement, stating that the relocated Japanese Canadians were "being spread all over Canada like the smallpox disease. ... This is a white man's country, and we want it left a white man's country."

The Universal Franchise, 1963
By the 1963 general election, held on October 8 that year, the last traces of racial and religious discrimination had been expunged from the law governing the federal franchise.

Prime Minister King denied that the policy was racist: a Japanese Canadian who had lived in Alberta before 1938 would not lose his vote, he argued, only a Japanese Canadian who moved there from British Columbia after 1938. The evacuees were "still citizens of British Columbia," he said, and subject to its laws even though they no longer lived in the province. (*Debates* July 17, 1944; 4912–4937)

After the Second World War, the most virulently anti-Japanese MPs lost their seats to more moderate members, and public opinion began to shift as well. Travel and other restrictions on Japanese Canadians continued until 1948, when Parliament deleted the reference to discrimination in the franchise on the basis of race. The discussion was brief, occupying just one column in the House of Commons debates for June 15, 1948. Although First Nations people would not be enfranchised for more than a decade, this particular form of racism in Canadian electoral law now belonged to history.

Religious Exclusions

Several religious groups were disenfranchised by the *War-time Elections Act* of 1917, mainly because they opposed military service. Most prominent among them were the Mennonites and the Doukhobors. This disenfranchisement ended with the end of the First World War, but the treatment later accorded the two groups in the development of the franchise varied enormously.

Mennonites migrating to Canada in the 1870s had been given an exemption from military service by an Order-in-Council dated March 3, 1873, but they lost the franchise during the First World War

Mr. King Goes to Ottawa
William Lyon Mackenzie King, prime minister from 1921 to 1926, 1926 to 1930 and 1935 to 1948, casts a ballot under the watchful eye of a deputy returning officer. Perhaps the photograph was posed, or maybe the DRO saw fit not to abide by the letter of the law concerning who should place the ballot in the box.

because they spoke an "enemy language" (German). They regained the vote when the *Dominion Elections Act* of 1920 superseded the *War-time Elections Act*.

The Mennonites attracted relatively little anti-alien hostility, as their way of life allowed them to blend into the farming communities where they lived. By contrast, the Hutterites and the Doukhobors aroused more animosity, not so much because of their pacifist beliefs, but because they practised communal farming. The Hutterites had migrated to Canada from the United States in 1918 to avoid conscription. Although they sparked some opposition locally where they settled, generally they attracted little notice, and they rarely voted.

The Doukhobors were another matter. In 1917, and again from 1934 to 1955 (when the ban on voting by conscientious objectors was lifted), Doukhobors lost the federal franchise, ostensibly because their faith forbade them to bear arms. The debates in the House of Commons showed clearly, however, that the MPs who opposed giving Doukhobors the vote were less concerned about military service than about the Doukhobors' social views and behaviour.

Debate on the 1934 *Dominion Elections Act* in particular revealed the fear and narrow-mindedness of some British Columbia MPs, in contrast with more widespread support for freedom of religion from MPs of other provinces.

W. J. Esling, the Conservative member for Kootenay West, stated that if MPs from other provinces had been in his constituency, they "would all have been quite willing to disenfranchise this religious sect."

Another Conservative MP, Grote Stirling, soon to be minister of national defence, said the Doukhobors behaved "with disgusting indecency." In particular, he resented the fact that they "voted Liberal en bloc," on the orders of their leader.

A. W. Neill, the Independent MP for Comox–Alberni, said that only "sickly sentimental" MPs wanted Doukhobors to have the franchise.

One of the MPs who did support the Doukhobors was J. S. Woodsworth, leader of the CCF. He praised the Doukhobors for their industriousness and protested against "religious tenets being made the basis for disfranchisement." Woodsworth and a number of Liberal MPs participating in the debate pointed out that the Doukhobors could hardly become good citizens if they and their descendants were disenfranchised.

So far as I know, citizenship in no country carries with it the right to vote. The right to vote is a conferred right in every case …

– Hon. Hugh Guthrie, Solicitor General
Debate on the *Dominion Elections Act*
House of Commons, April 29, 1920

Debating further revisions to the elections act in 1938, Esling, Stirling and Neill again opposed giving Doukhobors the vote. T. C. Love, provincial member for the region of British Columbia where the largest number of Doukhobors lived, claimed that giving them the vote would be the "end of true democracy in the West Kootenays." (*Vancouver Province*, April 7, 1938) The Doukhobors remained disenfranchised.

After the Second World War, as part of the general easing of racial and religious discrimination, racial disqualifications from the franchise were gradually dropped. In 1955, the last vestige of discrimination against a religious group in Canadian electoral law was repealed.

Aboriginal Peoples and the Franchise

Aboriginal peoples in Canada consist of First Nations, Inuit and Métis communities. Each has its own history and experience of the franchise.

First Nations people in most parts of Canada had the right to vote from Confederation on – but only if they gave up their status through a process defined in the *Indian Act* and known as "enfranchisement." Quite understandably, very few were willing to do this. It is worth noting that this requirement to give up status was not imposed on them if they joined the military. In fact, the franchise was extended to members of the First Nations who served in both world wars – although until 1924, any First World War veterans who returned to their reserves lost the right to vote. A great many First Nations people also served with distinction in the Canadian Forces during the Second World War, and this was among the reasons eventually leading Canadians to conclude that all Aboriginal people should have the full rights of citizenship.

Proposals to extend the franchise to First Nations date at least to 1885, when Status Indians in Eastern Canada who met the existing requirements gained the right to vote. This was revoked in 1898, and in general such proposals met a great deal of hostility. Isaac Burpee, MP for Saint John, said that the Indian knew no more of politics "than a child two years old," while another New Brunswick MP, A. H. Gillmor, the member for Charlotte, called the proposal to give Indians the vote "the crowning act of political rascality" on the part of Sir John A. Macdonald.

One reason for this opposition, apart from prevailing paternalistic or racist social attitudes, was the notion that First Nations people would become the dupes of non-First Nations politicians. Both Canada and the United States have a long tradition of newly enfranchised voters voting en bloc, often as directed by their community leaders. As these voters gained more education and became more integrated into North American society, they tended to drift away from the influence of political "bosses."

There was opposition to the franchise on the other side, as well. First Nations peoples had formed social groupings and elaborate systems of government well before their first contacts with Europeans. Many, therefore, looked unfavourably on nineteenth-century proposals for enfranchisement for at least two reasons: first, they perceived it as an end to their recognition as distinct nations or peoples and possibly the beginning of assimilation into non-First Nations society.

Second, voting in Canadian elections would mean participating in a system of government that was quite alien to the traditions, conventions and practices of governance of many First Nations peoples. Furthermore, electoral participation would have been essentially redundant – they already

Access to the Vote

Before the 1993 extension of the special ballot to anyone unable to vote at a polling station, making voting accessible throughout Canada's vast land mass often required extensive travel on the part of election officials.

had their own systems for choosing leaders and governing themselves.

In short, First Nations people were unenthusiastic about having the right to vote if it meant giving up their individual and group identities. Thus, until the government of Canada extended the vote to "Indian persons" unconditionally in 1960, there is little evidence that First Nations people wanted it or sought it.

For almost a century after the 1885 debate, there was little pressure to extend the franchise to

Elections in the North
The advent of modern communications technology, along with changes in the law such as the special ballot for mail-in registration and voting, has facilitated the task of conducting elections in the North and in other sparsely populated parts of the country for voters, candidates and election officials.

First Nations citizens, though it was granted in 1924 to First Nations veterans of the First World War, including veterans living on reserves. With the exception of those veterans, *The Dominion Franchise Act* of 1934 explicitly disqualified First Nations persons living on reserves and Inuit people from voting in federal elections.

Inuit Canadians had the vote restored to them without qualification in 1950. Among other strategies to protect its sovereignty in the Arctic following the Second World War and the onset of the Cold War, the Canadian government relocated individuals, families and communities into the high Arctic in the 1950s. At the same time, the government also extended, once again, the right to vote and all rights of citizenship to the Inuit. Until the early 1960s, however, they were rarely enumerated for federal elections. Most were geographically isolated well into the twentieth century, so in the absence of special efforts to enable them to vote, they had no means to exercise the franchise. In fact, it was only in the 1962 federal election that ballot boxes were finally placed in all Inuit communities in the eastern Arctic, thus permitting full exercise of the franchise. (Milen, 5)

The Métis, on the other hand, were treated as having the same rights as all other Canadians with respect to voting; thus, they never experienced any legislative impediments to the exercise of the franchise. Moreover, few Métis were covered by treaties or a federal statute like the *Indian Act*, so there was no basis on which to attempt to justify disqualifying them. In fact, the Métis in Manitoba exercised the right to vote as far back as 1873, when they voted to elect Louis Riel to Parliament.

A parliamentary committee recommended in 1948 that First Nations people be given the vote. The chairman of the Indian affairs committee said that

> a great step would be taken toward the assimilation of the Indian into the population of the Dominion of Canada, and it would make not only Indians but the other Canadians realize that we are all united.

But it was not until John Diefenbaker became prime minister that the franchise was extended with no strings attached. Diefenbaker had long advocated extending the vote to First Nations people. In his

The right to vote is one of the great privileges of democratic society, for after all it is you the people, not the Gallup poll, who determine into whose hands the guidance of public affairs may best be entrusted.

– John G. Diefenbaker
June 15, 1962

A Question of Rights
John George Diefenbaker, prime minister from 1957 to 1963, achieved a long-held personal goal when Parliament extended the franchise to registered Indians in 1960 with no strings attached. They were no longer required to give up their Indian status in order to vote.

memoirs, he described how, as a child growing up in Saskatchewan, he had met many Indians and had committed himself to getting them the right to vote. (Diefenbaker, 29–30) In 1958, Diefenbaker appointed James Gladstone (Akay Na-Muka, or "Many Guns") to the Senate, where he was the first member of First Nations origin.

On March 10, 1960, after a debate marked by virtually unanimous support, the House of Commons finally gave First Nations people the vote without forcing them to give up their status in exchange. In 1968, the first Status Indian elected to the House of Commons was Len Marchand, representing the British Columbia constituency of Kamloops–Cariboo. More First Nations people have been elected since then, though by no means in proportion to their presence in the Canadian population.

Status Indian women experienced a different and more complex history. Under the *Indian Act*, until 1985, an Indian groom conferred status on his non-Indian wife upon marriage, while the Indian bride of a non-Indian or a non-Status Indian man lost her status, as did any children of the marriage. They could no longer live on-reserve and lost the right to own reserve land or inherit family property; they could not receive treaty benefits or participate in band councils and political or social affairs in the community, and they lost the right to be buried in cemeteries with their ancestors.* However, they could decide to vote or not in a federal election without further concerns about loss of status. On June 28, 1985, Parliament passed Bill C-31, *An Act to amend the Indian Act*, which, among other things, removed this form of discrimination against First Nations women.

*Persistent challenges to this unfair law began with Mary Two-Axe Earley in 1967. Others followed in her footsteps. In February 1973, the cases of Jeannette Corbiere Lavell and Yvonne Bédard, both women who lost their Indian status by marrying non-Indian men, were heard together by the Supreme Court of Canada. On August 27, 1973, the Court delivered a 5-4 majority decision that the Bill of Rights did not apply to that section of the *Indian Act*, and the legislation was upheld. A similar case was brought before the United Nations Human Rights Committee in 1977 by Sandra Lovelace, who was appointed to the Canadian Senate in 2005. In 1981, the Committee found Canada in breach of the International Covenant on Civil and Political Rights.

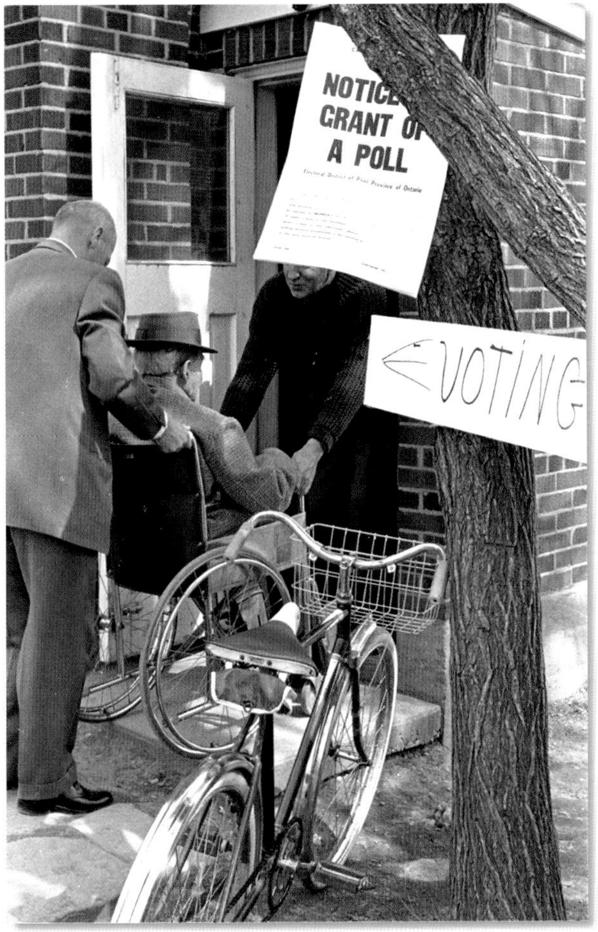

Restricted Right
By the 1963 general election, most legal restrictions on the franchise had been removed, but a voter with a disability might still face physical barriers to the polling station.

In each of the instances just recounted – extension of the vote to Canadians of Japanese and Chinese origin, to the Doukhobors and to First Nations people – change was accomplished by amending the existing electoral law. Such advances in the franchise might have been trumpeted as great achievements in human and democratic rights. For instance, J. W. Pickersgill, minister of citizenship and immigration in the previous Liberal government, suggested adoption of a special act to solemnize the 1960 enfranchisement of on-reserve Indians. But Ellen Fairclough, Canada's first female Cabinet member, who was charged with seeing the amendments through the House, said that this would be "merely gilding the lily," or in other words, unnecessary. (*Debates* March 10, 1960; 1957) In the more than 45 years since the unconditional right to vote was granted to all indigenous peoples in Canada, many voters from First Nations, Métis and Inuit communities have recognized the importance of federal electoral participation and have exercised their right to vote.

Accessibility and the Electoral Process

Mechanisms to ensure that electors could exercise their franchise multiplied in this period. In 1948, for example, time off from work to vote was increased to three hours. This rose to four hours in 1970, before settling back at three hours in 1996, when polling hours were extended, making the extra time off unnecessary.

A greater change in voting procedures was the postal ballot for members of the armed forces. The Mackenzie King government instituted the system for military personnel serving overseas during the Second World War, allowing some 342,000 members of the armed forces to vote in the 1945 general election.

For the same election, proxy voting was introduced for Canadians being held as prisoners of war. Proxy votes, some 1,300 in 1945, were cast by the nearest relatives of those being held prisoner. The provision was restored in 1951 and used again during the Korean conflict, when 18 Canadians were prisoners of war.

Voting by people who were away from home on election day was accommodated by several innovative procedures in this period. In 1951, special arrangements were introduced in sanatoriums and chronic care hospitals. Voting at polling stations set up in these locations, and in homes for the elderly after 1960, would be suspended temporarily so that election officers (with permission from those in charge of the facility) could take the voting equipment from room to room, enabling anyone who was bedridden to vote if he or she wished to do so.

In addition, the military postal ballot was extended to the spouses of armed forces personnel in 1955, so that they could vote while accompanying their husbands or wives on a posting away from the home constituency.

Exercising a Right

In the 1970s and 1980s, as public awareness of voters' diverse abilities and needs grew, better access for people with disabilities was achieved at many polling stations through administrative measures, but it was not until 1992 (Bill C-78) that the law was changed to require level access at polling stations.

Advanced Practices

Any voter who finds it more convenient can vote at an advance poll, held on the Friday, Saturday and Monday in the week before an election. Before 1960, voters could take advantage of advance polls only if they had one of the occupations specified in the law. A Progressive Conservative government, believing it had been disadvantaged by a summer election in 1953, introduced an amendment in 1960 allowing voters to use an advance poll, provided they swore an oath that they would be away from home on election day. The oath was dropped in 1977.

Consolidation and Review, 1961–1981

By 1960, then, amendments to Canada's electoral law had resulted in significant advances over the situation in 1920: racial and religious discrimination was no longer a factor in voter qualification, and no major group was deprived of the franchise deliberately or directly. The most significant changes in the law were concerned mainly with refining the electoral process – changes that affected how the process worked, rather than the extent or nature of the franchise.

Among these modifications were recognition of political parties in the law and the appointment of impartial commissions to set new constituency boundaries to reflect demographic change. Both changes had significant effects on the electoral process; but from an elector's perspective, the most discernible result was probably the appearance of candidates' party affiliations on the ballot and the opportunity to make a tax-deductible political contribution.

This period also saw numerous changes undertaken to meet the varying needs of electors, including extension of advance voting provisions to all voters, adjustments to voters lists and reduction of the voting age from 21 years to 18. In addition, this was a time when the rights and concerns of people with disabilities began to gain greater public recognition, resulting in changes in their access to the polls and privacy in casting their ballots. Finally, the passage in 1969 of the *Official Languages Act* meant that voters everywhere gained the right to have access to election materials in either English or French.

Advance Voting

When first introduced in 1920, voting at advance polls had been limited to only a few classes of voters. Advance voting was extended to members of the Royal Canadian Mounted Police and the armed forces in 1934, and to members of the military reserves in 1951. In each case, a voter at an advance poll had to swear on oath that he or she would be away on business on election day.

The election of 1953 was held in August, when many potential voters were on vacation. Turnout was only 68 percent, compared with 75 percent in the June 1949 election and 75 percent in the June 1957 election. The Progressive Conservatives felt that they had been especially hard hit by this.* After they gained power at the 1957 election, the advance vote was extended to all electors who

***Debates* January 27, 1954; 1515. J.W. Pickersgill, replying for the Liberals, said that "if there are a great number of Canadians who value their holidays more than their franchise, that does not mean they were disfranchised."

had reason to believe they would be absent from their polling division on election day and therefore unable to vote. Electors still had to swear an affidavit, however, under this 1960 amendment to the act. At the next general election – in 1962 – voter response was remarkable. The number of advance votes rose from an average of 10,000 in previous elections to nearly 100,000.

In 1977, the requirement to swear an affidavit was dropped. At the same time, a provision was introduced allowing people to vote at the returning office during the electoral period if they could not vote at an advance poll or on election day.

In 1993, voting in advance became more widely available when a provision was introduced permitting any elector to vote at the advance polls. Advance voting was no longer restricted to those who would be absent on election day.

Elections Canada

CONFIRMATION OF REGISTRATION

GENERAL ELECTION 1997 ÉLECTION GÉNÉRALE 1997

Élections Canada

CONFIRMATION D'INSCRIPTION

This confirms that the person named below is registered to vote.

L'inscription de la personne mentionnée ci-dessous est confirmée.

MAIL POSTE
Lettermail Poste-lettres
01094661 98

If the name or address shown is incorrect, or if an elector in your household did not receive a card, **CALL THE NUMBER ON THE BACK.**

S'il y a une erreur dans le nom ou l'adresse, ou si un électeur de votre domicile n'a pas reçu de carte, **APPELEZ AU NUMÉRO FIGURANT AU VERSO.**

AFFIX LABEL HERE - APPOSER L'ÉTIQUETTE ICI

Voter Notification

As we have seen, the 1934 provision requiring that a postcard be sent to each registered elector proved too expensive. Instead, voters were sent a copy of the list of electors for their poll. This system continued for several decades, but by the 1970s, many voters were objecting to what they considered an unacceptable invasion of privacy – in particular, women living alone and people who thought their occupation or the identity of the members of their households was no one's business but their own. There were also concerns that the lists – which together contained the names, addresses and occupations of the adults in every household in the country – could be used for other than electoral purposes.

In 1982, this provision was therefore dropped from the act. Instead, in a move reminiscent of 1934, each registered elector would receive a postcard confirming registration and showing where to vote; technological change had made this approach much more feasible and affordable than it had been in 1934. Electors who did not receive a card would know that they had to take steps to register if they wanted to vote.

Opening Up the Process

In the largest expansion of the vote since women were enfranchised in 1918, people between the ages of 18 and 20 got the vote in 1970 and used it for the first time in the 1972 election. Although reducing the voting age to 18 expanded the electorate considerably – by some two million young people in all – this change was not quite like removing religious or racial discrimination from the electoral law. Unlike extension of the franchise to racial

Everything Old Is New Again

First introduced in the 1930s but abandoned as too expensive and time-consuming, the postcard system of voter notification was made feasible in the 1980s by technological advances. In 1982, postcards replaced the public posting of electoral lists, a practice that raised privacy concerns, among others.

and religious minorities, lowering the voting age aroused relatively little controversy. It was the 1970s, the youth culture was at its height, and a general opening up of social and political life had begun as the politics of participation took hold.

This same social climate gave rise to greater recognition of the rights of voters with disabilities and others who might be excluded from voting for reasons related to physical abilities or illness. This recognition produced some legislative change, but for the most part, voters' special needs were addressed through administrative measures that were later incorporated into the law. Thus, for example, a 1977 amendment to the law introduced transfer certificates, allowing electors to vote at an advance poll with level access if their own was inaccessible. At the same time, throughout the 1970s, polling stations were located increasingly in public places, so that level access became more widely available. Special templates were also devised so that voters who were blind or visually impaired could preserve the secrecy of the vote, casting their ballots without assistance. These administrative arrangements became part of the law in 1992.

Proxy voting was extended twice in this period – to fishermen, sailors and prospectors in 1970, along with people who were ill or had physical disabilities, and to airplane crews, forestry and mapping teams, and trappers in 1977. In 1993, proxy voting was repealed when the use of special ballots under the Special Voting Rules was expanded.

A third set of changes opened the vote to certain classes of electors living abroad. In 1970, public servants, mainly diplomats, and their dependants posted outside Canada became eligible to use the Special Voting Rules – previously available only

From Far and Wide ...
Since 1993, voting by special ballot has enabled electors away from home on election day – including anyone travelling or living abroad temporarily – to vote by mail. An ingenious system of envelopes within envelopes enables election officials to assure the integrity of the vote (so that no one votes more than once, for example), while also preserving the secrecy of each voter's choice.

Voting from Anywhere
By applying for a kit like this one, an elector who cannot go to the polling station can register to vote and cast a ballot by mail. The special ballot is especially helpful for Canadians temporarily living abroad or travelling during an election campaign.

to military personnel and their dependants. Civilian employees of the military (usually teachers and administrative support staff at schools on Canadian Forces bases) gained this eligibility in 1977. But, until 1993, ordinary Canadians who happened to be away from home and unable to vote, either on polling day or at advance polls, still could not cast a ballot.

After the adoption of the *Official Languages Act* in 1969, Elections Canada implemented a policy to ensure that electors were served in their official language in constituencies where at least 5 percent of the population spoke the minority official language. From the early 1990s onward, this service was ensured across Canada.

One slight narrowing of the franchise occurred in this period. In 1970, the law was amended to provide that British subjects who had not adopted Canadian citizenship would be disqualified from voting unless they took out citizenship by 1975. Before then, British subjects were qualified electors, but they had to be "ordinarily resident in Canada."

Distributing Election Supplies
In the 1950s, some 50,000 packages of election supplies were shipped to returning officers across Canada at each general election. Today, the number of parcels has reached 110,000.

CHAPTER 4

The Charter Era 1982–2006

No doubt the most significant influence on electoral law in the post-war years was the adoption of the *Canadian Charter of Rights and Freedoms*, which came into effect on April 17, 1982.

SECTIONS 2 TO 5 of the Charter set out fundamental freedoms and democratic rights. Under section 3:

> Every citizen of Canada has the right to vote in an election of members of the House of Commons or of a legislative assembly [of a province or territory] and to be qualified for membership therein.

Many Canadians probably assumed that their right to vote was assured well before 1982. As we have seen throughout this book, however, many people had been denied the franchise – some on racial or religious grounds, others because they could not get to a poll on voting day. Even when improvements in election law were proposed – for instance, extending advance polling to groups other than railway workers and commercial travellers – they sometimes provoked resistance in Parliament. We have seen, for example, how it took 50 years to extend advance voting to everyone who wanted it; each time a new group was given the "privilege" of advance voting, there was opposition, generally on the basis of cost or administrative convenience. Arguments based on democratic rights and principles were heard less often.

The Charter signalled a different approach. Section 2 guarantees the right to freedom of thought, expression and association, while section 1 ensures that the Charter rights and freedoms are subject only to "such reasonable limits prescribed by law as can be demonstrably justified in a free and democratic society." Moreover, the section 3 right to vote cannot be overridden by legislatures under any circumstance (as can some other Charter provisions by means of the so-called notwithstanding clause*).

The Charter also provides a basis on which to challenge losses or infringements of rights. Someone denied the franchise, for example, could appeal to the courts; if the appeal were successful, the courts might strike down part of the law or require changes in the administrative rules that resulted in disenfranchisement – and this has indeed happened frequently since 1982. Since the introduction of the Charter, there have been over 30 court cases

*Under subsection 33(1) of the Charter: "Parliament or the legislature of a province may expressly declare in an Act of Parliament or of the legislature, as the case may be, that the Act or a provision thereof shall operate notwithstanding a provision included in section 2 or sections 7 to 15 of this Charter." Thus, while the fundamental freedoms specified under section 2, and the legal and equality rights outlined in sections 7 to 15, can in some instances be overridden, the democratic right to vote guaranteed under section 3 is indelibly protected.

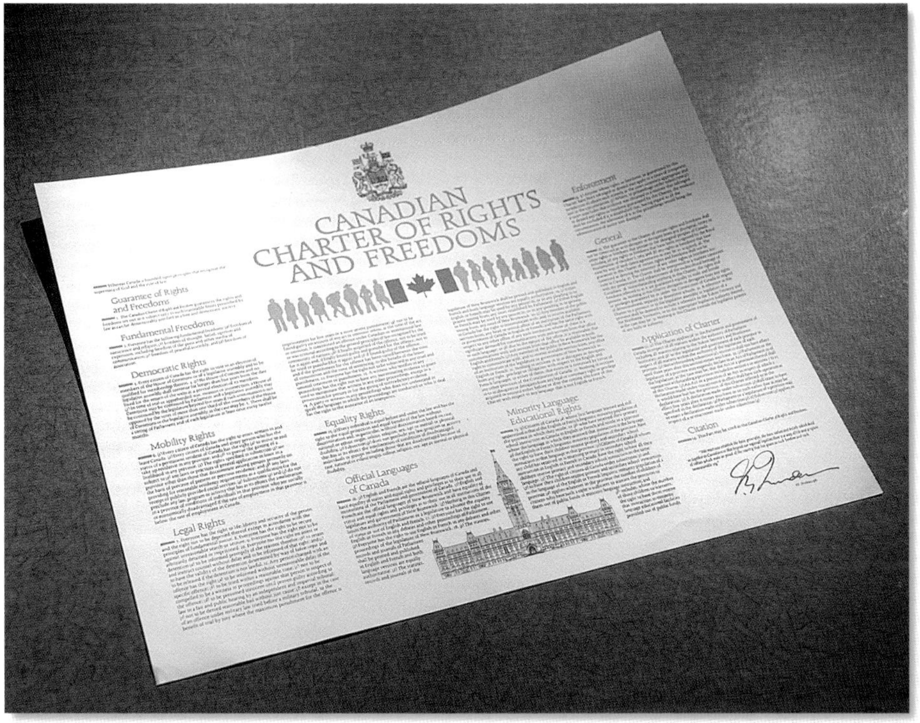

A Democratic Right
The right to vote and to be a candidate for office has been enshrined since 1982 in the *Canadian Charter of Rights and Freedoms*. The Charter provided a basis for several groups to challenge their exclusion from the franchise and to contest other election law provisions in the courts.

involving electoral matters. Apart from the *Criminal Code*, federal electoral legislation is without a doubt among the laws most often challenged on the basis of the constitutional rights and freedoms established by the Charter.

Significant advances in election law and administration had occurred before the advent of the Charter – denial of the franchise on the basis of gender, religion, race, ethnicity and income had been removed from the law, and administrative steps had been taken to improve access to the vote for people with disabilities, people away from home on election day and members of the public service and the military serving abroad.

Yet, notwithstanding the changes to electoral law since the Second World War, disqualifications remained for judges, prisoners, expatriates and people with mental disabilities, and some people were still administratively disenfranchised. In addition, some citizens' electoral participation had also been curtailed: civil servants in some jurisdictions, for example, were prohibited from engaging in activities that would reveal partisan preferences.

At the same time, there was mounting interest in addressing public perceptions of influence peddling, stemming from the fact that the financial activities of political parties and third-party advocates were essentially unregulated. Yet the efforts to appease such perceptions, by adding restrictions on electoral financing to the *Canada Elections Act*, also fuelled numerous Charter-based court challenges, with alleged infringements of the right to freedom of expression – guaranteed under section 2 of the Charter – being the most commonly cited cause for legal recourse. As well, restrictions on broadcasting, third-party advertising and the publication of opinion polls during election campaigns faced similar tests under the section 2 guarantees.

Nonetheless, step by step, since 1982, many of these problems have been addressed. Measures taken by Parliament and by election officials ensure that Canada's electoral process is not only legally but also administratively consistent with Charter principles – making the vote accessible to everyone entitled to cast a ballot, while protecting the integrity of the process by balancing the influence of money on electoral contests with the right to free speech.

The achievement of these ends was assisted by the Royal Commission on Electoral Reform and Party Financing (also known as the Lortie Commission). It was appointed by the federal government in 1989 to review, among other matters, the many anomalies in the electoral process identified by Charter challengers. In 1992, the Commission's recommendations were reviewed by the Hawkes Committee, a special eight-member panel that produced additional recommendations concerning the *Canada Elections Act*. Both reports were reviewed by Parliament, with advice and support from the Chief Electoral Officer. One of the outcomes was the passage of Bill C-78 in 1992 and Bill C-114 in 1993 – which together initiated significant changes in the way electoral law dealt with access to the vote. Another was a host of recommendations by the Chief Electoral Officer that paved the way for major reforms to electoral finance regulation (most notably through Bill C-24 in 2003).

This chapter shows clearly the pervasive influence of Charter challenges on the development of these and other key pieces of electoral legislation.

Bill C-114: *An Act to amend the Canada Elections Act*

Among its many broad-ranging amendments to the *Canada Elections Act* in 1993, Bill C-114:

- extended the right to register on election day to electors from both rural and urban areas
- extended the use of the special ballot, enabling any elector to register and vote without having to appear in person on election day or at an advance poll
- permitted any elector to vote at an advance poll
- removed voting disqualifications for judges, people with mental disabilities and inmates serving less than two years in correctional institutions
- restricted election advertising expenses to $1,000 for "third parties" (that is, persons or groups other than candidates and political parties). Restricted expenses were those incurred for the purpose of supporting or opposing, directly and during an election, a particular registered party or the election of a particular candidate.

Election Administration and the Charter

Elections Canada ushered in the era of the Charter with Jean-Marc Hamel as Chief Electoral Officer, who began the process of responding to the Charter's rapidly burgeoning impact on the *Canada Elections Act* during the last eight years of his tenure. By the time Jean-Pierre Kingsley was appointed in 1990, a dozen or so cases had already come before the courts to challenge the act on Charter grounds. This unprecedented stream of legal challenges to federal legislation gave the new Chief Electoral Officer an opportunity not afforded his predecessor: foreknowledge of the Charter's sweeping effect on how Canadian legislation would henceforth be conceived, interpreted and executed.

In Mr. Kingsley's assessment, the Charter – along with developments in technology and the growing global interest in democracy – had fundamentally changed the function of his Office. Serving the public trust demanded more than simply administering the electoral legislation – it demanded an approach that was strategic and proactive. As the politically independent custodian of the *Canada Elections Act*, the Chief Electoral Officer was in a unique position to help legislators mould its provisions into conformity with the rights and freedoms set out in the Charter, while retaining the spirit of the act.

In 1990, Elections Canada faced a number of challenges. It employed a management system that functioned on a case-by-case basis. It faced a pending increase in the number of electoral

Signing the Writs

The Chief Electoral Officer of Canada, Jean-Pierre Kingsley, signed 308 writs, one for each electoral district, for the general election of June 28, 2004. At each election, a document like this instructs every returning officer to conduct an election to choose a member of Parliament.

districts following the 1991 census, and the need to implement recommendations from the Lortie Commission that included a means for expatriate Canadians to vote and a permanent register of electors. On top of these demands, the 35th general election was imminent, and there was the distinct possibility of a federal referendum. The concurrent information technology boom could have relieved many of these pressures, had the organization not also found itself significantly challenged in that area.

To address these problems, as well as the needs of a significantly enlarged organization, a number of measures were implemented that reshaped the way elections are administered. Today, for example, Elections Canada employs a planning-based management system, and virtually all aspects of electoral operations have been computerized.

Election Administration and Access to the Ballot

Charter Enfranchisements

To date, the principal beneficiaries of Charter challenges to electoral law, as far as the right to vote is concerned, have been judges, prisoners and people with mental disabilities.

Judges appointed by the federal Cabinet had been legally disqualified from voting since 1874. The law remained in place until 1993, but a Charter-based court ruling at the time of the 1988 general election rendered the provision inoperative. About 500 federally appointed judges became eligible to cast ballots in federal elections after a court struck down the relevant section of the *Canada Elections Act*, declaring it contrary to the Charter's guarantee of the right to vote.

Prisoners had not been allowed to vote since 1898 – although according to at least one MP, Lucien Cannon, some inmates appear to have found a way around the rules:

> I know a case where the prisoners were allowed, under a sheriff's guard, to go and register their votes and they came back afterwards.
>
> Debates *April 19, 1920; 1820*

The solicitor general of the day appeared not to credit this story, replying that prisoners might be on voters lists, but since they could not get to a ballot box, they would be disenfranchised in any event.

Until 1982, there was little parliamentary support for ensuring that prisoners could exercise the right to vote. Since 1982, however, inmates of several penal institutions have relied on the

Charter to establish through the courts that they should indeed be able to vote. They began by challenging provincial election laws, where they had some success. Then, during the 1988 federal election, the Manitoba Court of Appeal ruled that the judiciary should not be determining which prisoners should or should not be disenfranchised; this was a matter for legislators, not judges.

Since then, judicial opposition to a general disqualification of prisoners has been demonstrated in various court decisions. These cases determined that a general or blanket disqualification of all inmates would no longer be tolerated under the Charter, but the courts did not establish what specific disqualifications would be acceptable, leaving that decision to legislators.

In 1993, Parliament removed from the law the disqualification for prisoners serving sentences of less than two years, but for prisoners serving longer terms, the disqualification remained in effect.

The new provision was challenged by an inmate serving a longer sentence. In its decision in *Sauvé v. Canada (Chief Electoral Officer)* in 2002, the Supreme Court of Canada ruled that prisoners serving terms of more than two years could not be disqualified from voting, stating that legislation infringing on prisoners' right to vote was not a reasonable limit of that right.

Although the legislation has not been amended, the Charter has, given the Supreme Court's ruling, secured access to the vote for all prisoners.

In the 1980s and early 1990s, several changes in election administration and the law made it significantly easier for electors with physical disabilities to vote. One group of people with disabilities remained explicitly disenfranchised, however – those who were "restrained of [their]

Denying the right to vote does not comply with the requirements [...] that punishment must not be arbitrary and must serve a valid criminal law purpose. Absence of arbitrariness requires that punishment be tailored to the acts and circumstances of the individual offender.

– Supreme Court of Canada
Decision in *Sauvé v. Canada*
October 31, 2002

The Courts and the Charter

The Supreme Court of Canada and several provincial courts, in interpreting the rights guaranteed in the *Canadian Charter of Rights and Freedoms*, have made a number of rulings on provisions of the *Canada Elections Act*. Court rulings have affected the definition of who has the right to vote, the number of candidates required for a political party to qualify for registration, limits on the publishing of election surveys during a campaign period and spending by third parties.

Prisoners and the Vote: *Sauvé v. Canada*

1992 *Sauvé v. Canada* challenged a long-standing provision in the *Canada Elections Act* that prohibited inmates from voting. In its decision, the Ontario Court of Appeal considered three objectives that might be deemed important enough to infringe on prisoners' right to vote:

- affirming and maintaining the sanctity of the franchise in our democracy
- preserving the integrity of the voting process
- sanctioning offenders

The Ontario Court of Appeal ruled that, even if taken collectively, these objectives could not justify outright denial of voting rights. The federal prohibition on inmate voting was repealed. The timing of the decision enabled inmates to vote during the 1992 federal referendum on the Charlottetown Accord.

1993 The Supreme Court of Canada upheld the *Sauvé* (1992) verdict, stating that the act's prohibition against inmate voting was too broad, failing to meet the requirement that penal sanctions must result in minimal impairment of Charter rights, and that the negative effects of impairing the right must be proportionate to the benefits.

That same year, Bill C-114 removed the voting exclusion for prisoners serving less than two years.

1995 In *Sauvé* (1995), the Federal Court Trial Division accepted the government's argument that enhancing civic responsibility, respect for the law and penal sanctions were sufficiently important objectives to warrant infringement of a Charter right. It found, however, that the disqualification for inmates serving two years or more still failed the tests of both proportionality and minimum impairment. Successful administration of the inmate vote in the 1992 referendum also appears to have influenced the Court's decision to strike down the prisoner voting restrictions of Bill C-114.

1999 The Federal Court of Appeal reversed *Sauvé* (1995), ruling that Bill C-114's voting disqualification for inmates serving two years or more did meet the minimum impairment and proportionality tests.

2002 On appeal, the Supreme Court of Canada upheld *Sauvé* (1995), concluding that:

- denying individuals the right to vote will not educate them in the values of community and democracy
- a blanket disenfranchisement is an inappropriate punishment because it is not related to the nature of the individual crime
- disenfranchisement does not increase democratic respect because it denies individuals' inherent dignity

2004 Parliament did not amend the *Canada Elections Act* to remove the voting disqualification for inmates serving over two years. Nevertheless, the Chief Electoral Officer applied the *Sauvé* (2002) decision during the 2004 and 2006 general elections, giving all inmates the opportunity to vote.

liberty of movement or deprived of the management of [their] property by reason of mental disease." In 1985, a Commons committee recommended that they be enumerated and have the same right to vote as other Canadians, and the Lortie Commission reached a similar conclusion in its 1992 report.

In the meantime, the courts struck down the provision. In 1988, the Canadian Disability Rights Council argued in a Charter challenge that the *Canada Elections Act* should not disqualify people who were under some form of restraint because of a mental disability. The Court agreed, although the ruling did not specify what level of mental competence would qualify a voter. In 1993, Parliament removed disqualification on the basis of mental disability as part of Bill C-114.

Accessibility of the Vote

Throughout the 1980s, the disability rights movement in Canada pushed for legislative reform to enable full and equal access to all federal programs for people with physical disabilities. While, before Bill C-114, people with mental disabilities were explicitly excluded from voting, those with physical disabilities faced a similar implicit disenfranchisement, as numerous features of the legislation made voting physically impractical for many electors.

By the early 1990s, the matter had caught Parliament's attention on several fronts. A report entitled *A Consensus for Action: The Economic Integration of Disabled Persons*, published by the Standing Committee on Human Rights and the Status of Disabled Persons in June 1990, proposed a mandatory review across all federal departments, agencies and Crown corporations to identify all legislation that presented a barrier to people with physical disabilities. The Honourable Robert René de Cotret, Minister responsible for the status of persons with disabilities, initiated the review that fall.

From Metal to Cardboard

Recyclable cardboard ballot boxes first replaced the traditional metal ones at the 1988 general election (in Quebec and Ontario) and at the 1992 federal referendum in the rest of the country. Developed by the National Research Council at Elections Canada's request, the cardboard boxes are lightweight and economical to produce. They can be shipped flat for easy assembly by polling station staff as needed, eliminating the need to store more than 100,000 boxes between elections. The cardboard voting screens were also redesigned to include an upper flap, which increases privacy and protects the secrecy of the vote.

Removing Barriers to Voting
Obstacles, the 1981 report of the House of Commons Special Committee on the Disabled and the Handicapped, showed there were still many barriers to voting. The Committee recommended that Canada "establish a postal vote system" similar to the one in Manitoba and that the Chief Electoral Officer accommodate "the mobility problems of disabled persons." Another recommendation suggested amending the *Canada Elections Act* to "include provision for special polls at hospitals and nursing homes." These measures were included when Parliament passed Bill C-78 in 1992 and Bill C-114 in 1993, although the Chief Electoral Officer had already taken some administrative steps toward those goals. Among several clauses to improve accessibility, Bill C-78 provided for level access at all polling stations, and Bill C-114 extended special ballot voting to all electors.

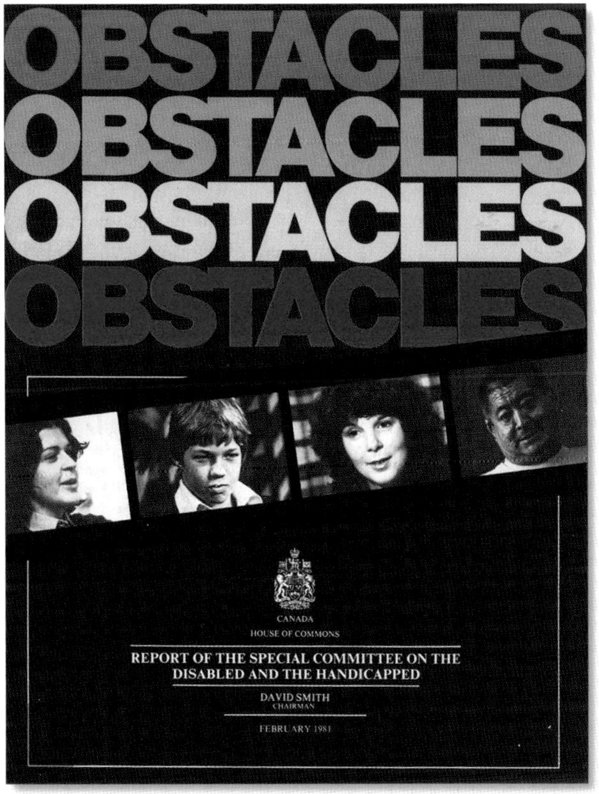

Meanwhile, the idea of creating an omnibus bill to enact simultaneous cross-legislative amendments in the area of disability had acquired momentum from various disability rights organizations as well as from the July 1990 passage of the *Americans with Disabilities Act* in the United States. Community groups for persons with disabilities coordinated their response to the proposed changes in federal legislation through the Canadian Disability Rights Council, which submitted its own legislative proposals to the secretary of state in September 1991. Based on those proposals, together with the work of the Standing Committee, and additional recommendations from the Lortie Commission, the Hawkes Committee and the Chief Electoral Officer, de Cotret introduced Bill C-78: *An Act to amend certain Acts with respect to persons with disabilities*. Parliament's subsequent passage of the bill effected sweeping revisions to six federal acts.

Bill C-78 marked the first time in some years that Parliament had enacted legislation dealing exclusively with the concerns of Canadians with disabilities. It was also the first time such reforms were devised through direct consultation with the disability community – a significant reason why the bill was generally well received by those affected.

One among Bill C-78's many important reforms was a specific mandate for the Chief Electoral Officer to initiate public education and information programs to make the electoral process better known to the public – especially those most likely to experience difficulties exercising the franchise, whether because of disabilities, language barriers or other factors.

While Bill C-78 focused on the needs of Canadians with disabilities, other legislation during this period improved access to the vote for all Canadians. In 1993, Bill C-114 effectively replaced proxy voting with an extension of the Special Voting Rules so that all electors could use the special ballot to vote by mail or in the office of the returning officer. The special ballot is a registration and voting system for Canadians away from their home ridings, people with disabilities, prison inmates and any other elector who cannot vote in person on election day or at an advance poll. All Canadians living or travelling outside the country – not just military personnel and diplomats – could now vote, provided that they had not been absent

Bill C-78: *An Act to amend certain Acts with respect to persons with disabilities*

Bill C-78 (1992) made a number of amendments to electoral law and administration that made voting more accessible to persons with disabilities.

- It provided for mobile polling stations at institutions where seniors and persons with disabilities live. Election officers could take a ballot box to people who might have difficulty getting to the ordinary polling place.
- It guaranteed level access at all polling stations and the returning office; unavoidable exceptions would be permitted only with the authorization of the Chief Electoral Officer. Of the 17,684 polling sites in the 2006 general election, only 43 (0.2 percent) did not have level access, compared with 89 (0.5 percent) in the 2000 general election.
- It introduced transfer certificates that allow people with disabilities to vote at a different poll if their own does not have level access.
- It required templates to be available for the use of voters who are blind or have impaired vision.
- It enabled deputy returning officers to appoint language or sign language interpreters to assist them in communicating with electors.
- It allowed deputy returning officers to mark an elector's ballot on his or her behalf, in the presence of a witness, if the elector is unable to vote because of a physical disability.
- It mandated public education and information programs for Canadians with special needs.

Bringing the Ballot Box to Voters
In 1992, Bill C-78 made access to the vote easier in a number of ways. Among the improvements were mobile polling stations that serve many seniors and persons with disabilities in the institutions where they live.

Voting by Special Ballot
Any elector may now register and vote by mail or, as shown here, in person at the returning office. Those voting by special ballot use a unique system of three envelopes to preserve the secrecy of their choice.

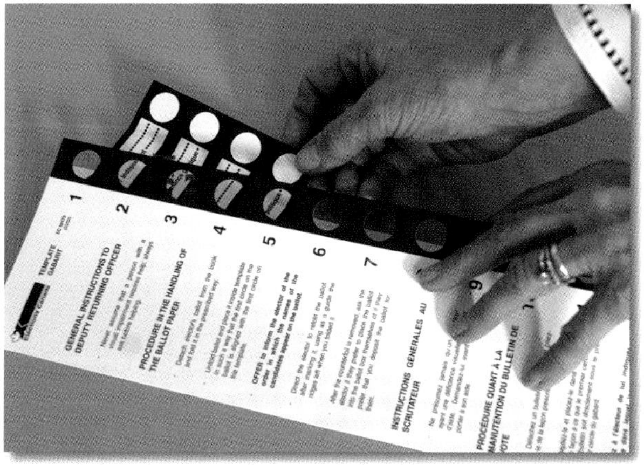

Accessibility for Voters with Visual Disabilities
Voters with visual disabilities can use a cardboard template that has a series of holes, one for each candidate. This template enables the voters to feel where to mark the ballot for the candidate they prefer.

Voting While Serving Far Away

Members of Canada's military are able to vote in a federal election, regardless of where in Canada they are stationed or whether they are serving in a foreign land. Canadian Forces members – including teachers and administrative support staff at armed forces schools outside Canada – vote by special ballot. For example, at Camp Julien, in Afghanistan, Canadians serving in the International Security Assistance Force received ballots and the list of candidates for the 2004 general election. They voted a few days before most Canadians so that their ballots could be sent back to Ottawa in time for counting.

from Canada for more than five years, intended to return home at some time and applied for the special ballot before the deadline.

Once advance voting became available to all citizens in 1993, Canadian voters increasingly took advantage of the early opportunity to cast a ballot. Before the change, just over 500,000 Canadians voted at advance polls during the 1988 general election. That number rose to 633,000 in 1993, and 704,000 in 1997. In 2000, 775,000 Canadians voted in advance; in 2004, that number rose to 1.2 million, and to 1.5 million in 2006.

For many years, the polls opened and closed on election day at a standard hour in every time zone across the country. Ballots would be counted as the polls closed in each time zone from east to west, but voters would learn the results from elsewhere in the country only when the polls closed in their time zone. In Western Canada, voters would often turn on their television sets after their polls had closed only to learn that the outcome of the election had already been decided by ballots counted in the rest of the country. This created the disconcerting perception that the Western vote had no bearing on the national result. In 1996, the *Canada Elections Act* was amended to introduce staggered voting hours on election day at a general election, so that results would be available at approximately the same time across the country.

In 2000, the act was further amended to empower the Chief Electoral Officer to adjust voting hours in regions that do not switch to daylight saving time. As well, voting hours for all by-elections held on the same day in the same time zone now run from 8:30 a.m. to 8:30 p.m., local time. For by-elections held on the same day but in different time zones, staggered voting hours apply.

Staggered Voting Hours
Canada's six time zones once created concern that Eastern ballots were counted and the results broadcast before some voters in Western Canada had finished casting their votes. The introduction of staggered voting hours in 2000 largely eliminated this problem, as the majority of election results from across the country are available at approximately the same time.

Staggered Voting Hours

In 1996, the times at which polls open and close in each time zone across Canada changed as follows:

Before staggered voting hours

Region	Local Time	Eastern Time
Newfoundland Time	9:00 a.m. – 8:00 p.m.	7:30 a.m. – 6:30 p.m.
Atlantic Time	9:00 a.m. – 8:00 p.m.	8:00 a.m. – 7:00 p.m.
Eastern Time	9:00 a.m. – 8:00 p.m.	9:00 a.m. – 8:00 p.m.
Central Time	9:00 a.m. – 8:00 p.m.	10:00 a.m. – 9:00 p.m.
Mountain Time	9:00 a.m. – 8:00 p.m.	11:00 a.m. – 10:00 p.m.
Pacific Time	9:00 a.m. – 8:00 p.m.	12:00 a.m. – 11:00 p.m.

After staggered (and extended) voting hours

Region	Local Time	Eastern Time
Newfoundland Time	8:30 a.m. – 8:30 p.m.	7:00 a.m. – 7:00 p.m.
Atlantic Time	8:30 a.m. – 8:30 p.m.	7:30 a.m. – 7:30 p.m.
Eastern Time	9:30 a.m. – 9:30 p.m.	9:30 a.m. – 9:30 p.m.
Central Time*	8:30 a.m. – 8:30 p.m.	9:30 a.m. – 9:30 p.m.
Mountain Time*	7:30 a.m. – 7:30 p.m.	9:30 a.m. – 9:30 p.m.
Pacific Time	7:00 a.m. – 7:00 p.m.	10:00 a.m. – 10:00 p.m.

*In Saskatchewan, when daylight saving time is in effect for the rest of the country, the following voting hours apply:

Region	Local Time	Eastern Time
Central Time	7:30 a.m. – 7:30 p.m.	9:30 a.m. – 9:30 p.m.
Mountain Time	7:00 a.m. – 7:00 p.m.	10:00 a.m. – 10:00 p.m.

Meanwhile, widespread use of the World Wide Web and e-mail presented new challenges respecting controls on the premature release of election results. When a resident of British Columbia named Paul Bryan was prosecuted for posting results of the 2000 general election from Eastern provinces before polls in the West had closed, he challenged the constitutionality of the prohibition as set out in section 329 of the *Canada Elections Act*. The Provincial Court of British Columbia ruled against him in a 2003 decision, stating that, while the prohibition did infringe on freedom of expression, the objective of electoral fairness made this infringement reasonable under section 1 of the Charter. The Supreme Court of British Columbia overturned the decision on appeal, however, ruling that the violation of freedom of expression took precedence over the objective of the act.

At that point, the Chief Electoral Officer applied the prohibition on the transmission of election results across the country. This decision was based on the desire to achieve fair application of the act across the country.

On appeal, in May 2005, the Court of Appeal for British Columbia upheld the constitutionality of the publication ban under section 1 of the Charter, noting the impossibility of measuring the consequences of the non-regulated transmission of election results.

Mr. Bryan's appeal was heard by the Supreme Court of Canada on October 16, 2006. As of the date of publication, the Court has not yet rendered a judgment.

The National Register of Electors

First broached in the 1930s, the subject of a permanent register of electors – to replace the long-standing door-to-door enumeration process – was revisited on several occasions.

In 1968, the Canadian Representation Commissioner considered the system of continuous registration used in Australia, but dismissed this as too costly.

The 1986 White Paper on Election Law Reform, which looked at both permanent lists and annual enumerations, ultimately recommended that the existing enumeration approach be retained. However, it also inspired further reflection on the subject by outlining several potential benefits of a permanent list, including shorter campaign periods and the sharing of enumeration results among municipal, provincial and federal jurisdictions.

In the end, it was the 1989 Auditor General's report – critical of Elections Canada for not yet using computer technology to streamline its operations – that motivated the push for the long-elusive permanent list.

Several by-elections during 1990 afforded the first opportunity to test customized software for computerized voters lists, which came to be known as the Elections Canada Automated Production of Lists of Electors (ECAPLE) system. In 1992, Elections Canada prepared computerized voters lists for the referendum on the Charlottetown Accord and formally launched ECAPLE in 220 electoral districts, excluding Quebec, where the 1992 referendum was conducted under provincial legislation. The *Referendum Act* was subsequently amended to permit the use of the 1992 voters lists for the 1993 general election. This election gave Elections Canada the opportunity to develop the revision procedures necessary to ensure quality when reusing an existing list. Further, in the 1993 election, ECAPLE was extended to include the 75 electoral districts in Quebec.

The idea of establishing a register of electors received great impetus from the recommendations of the Lortie Commission. In 1992, the Commission, judging conditions not yet right for establishing a federal register, recommended that provincial lists of electors be used for federal purposes.

In 1995, Elections Canada established a working group to look at the many technical, legal, financial and other issues involved in establishing a permanent register. The team's report, submitted to the Chief Electoral Officer in March 1996, indicated that such a register would be both feasible and cost-effective, could shorten the election period by eliminating enumeration and could significantly reduce costs and duplication of effort across Canada. By that autumn, with the advocacy of the Honourable Herb Gray, Leader of the Government in the House of Commons and Minister responsible for electoral reform, Parliament had drafted amendments to the *Canada Elections Act* to enable the necessary administrative changes. With the December passage of Bill C-63, the mandate to create Canada's National Register of Electors was finally granted.

In April 1997, in preparation for the 1997 general election, Elections Canada conducted its final door-to-door enumeration. Because provincial elections had recently been held in Alberta and Prince Edward Island, lists from those provinces were used for the 1997 preliminary lists of electors. The National Register of Electors became a reality after this enumeration and was used for the first time during the June 1997 election.

Since that enumeration, the Register has been updated regularly with data from a variety of sources, obtained through information-sharing agreements negotiated by the Chief Electoral Officer. Data-sharing partners of the Register include its provincial counterparts in British Columbia and Quebec, provincial and territorial motor vehicle and vital statistics registrars and, federally, the Canada Revenue Agency, Citizenship and Immigration Canada and Canada Post. Together, these sources update the addresses of the approximately three million Canadians who move each year, and identify the names of new electors who turn 18 years of age or acquire Canadian citizenship, and those who die and must be removed from the lists. Elections Canada also updates the Register from the electoral lists of the six provinces and territories that still use some form of enumeration, and the agency normally visits some 10 percent of households in targeted revision initiatives during federal elections. Both the *Canada Elections Act* and the *Privacy Act* protect voters' personal information.

From its conception, a primary goal of the National Register of Electors was to minimize duplication of effort between elections and across jurisdictions, thereby reducing costs for the taxpayer. According to a statement by the Chief Electoral Officer to the Standing Senate Committee on

The current approach assumes that an enumeration must be as complete as possible if voter registration is to achieve full coverage. This ignores the fact that revision and election-day registration are integral components of a comprehensive process of registration.

– Royal Commission on Electoral Reform
and Party Financing
Final Report, 1992

Registering at Home

While most information for the voters lists comes from the National Register of Electors, targeted revision of high mobility and low registration areas is conducted during election campaigns. Revising agents visit new subdivisions, apartment buildings, student residences, nursing homes and chronic care hospitals. The effectiveness of door-to-door canvassing is declining because increasing numbers of people are away from home during the day and there is growing reluctance to open doors to strangers.

National Finance on February 8, 2005, concerning its use in the 2000 and 2004 general elections, the Register was estimated to have "saved $31 million at the provincial and municipal levels, over and above the $60 million net savings at the federal level. If one includes British Columbia's projected $11 million savings [for the May 2005 provincial elections], the estimated total cost avoidance to date resulting from the National Register of Electors amounts to over $100 million." According to the report of the Chief Electoral Officer of British Columbia following the 2005 provincial general election, targeted revision in that province, which was supplemented with Register information from Elections Canada, was much more economical than the 1999 mail-based enumeration. In 1999, 28,000 voters were added, and there were just over 1 million registration transactions, at a total cost of more than $4 million. In 2005, Elections BC spent $3.2 million to add almost 650,000 voters and perform 3.6 million registration transactions.

By eliminating the need to conduct a full enumeration with each election, the Register enabled another change long advocated by many voters: the shortening of election campaigns. In 1997, the minimum length of time required between the issue of the election writs and polling day was reduced from 47 to 36 days, and this standard has remained in effect.

The 2000 Canada Elections Act

The majority of the federal electoral legislation in force at the end of the last century was enacted in 1970. In the 30 years following, the *Canada Elections Act* evolved into an intimidating maze of updates, amendments, revisions and clarifications, to the extent that much of its contents were hard to decipher. Additionally, several recommendation lists produced through the 1990s made it increasingly clear that the act was in need of much more than a bit of housecleaning. After the 1992 reports of the Lortie Commission and the Hawkes Committee, as well as much related input from the Chief Electoral Officer over the years, the Standing Committee on Procedure and House Affairs declared that the cumulative investment of effort in electoral reform demanded that Parliament make fixing the act a priority.

With the experience of the 1997 general election still fresh, the Committee tabled its own report the following June. Their synthesis of the previous work and recommendations made over the years provided the basis for the new legislation. With the passage of Bill C-2 in September 2000, the long-standing need to streamline the language, organization and provisions of the act had been met. A new *Canada Elections Act* was born.

In addition to simplifying the old legislation, the new act made significant changes to it, including better access to the ballot, regulating the publication of opinion polls and regulating election advertising by third parties.

Highlights of the 2000 *Canada Elections Act*

- The act has been reorganized and clarified to make it easier to interpret and apply.
- Regulation of election advertising expenses by third parties has been extended to include requirements for registration, disclosure and spending limits of $150,000 nationally – $3,000 in a particular electoral district – per general election. The spending limits are adjusted annually for inflation.
- The publication or broadcasting of election advertising and new election opinion surveys is prohibited on election day until all polling stations in the electoral district are closed.
- Disclosure of financial information by registered parties is subject to more rigorous reporting requirements.
- The Commissioner of Canada Elections is empowered to enter into compliance agreements and to seek injunctions during a campaign to require compliance with the act.
- The act provides for other administrative changes to improve the accessibility of Canada's electoral process.

In recent years, the *Canada Elections Act* has been amended several times to make access to voting easier, establish the National Register of Electors, conform more closely with the *Canadian Charter of Rights and Freedoms* and extend regulations governing political financing.

Registering at the Polls
Canadians who are not already on the voters lists can register when they go to vote at the advance or election day polls. They must present proof of their identity and residence; or they may swear a statement of that information if they are accompanied by another elector who is already registered and who vouches for them.

The act also made important new provisions for its own enforcement. For example, it allowed the Commissioner of Canada Elections (the person responsible for this enforcement) to resolve some contraventions by entering into compliance agreements – a remedial rather than a punitive measure. Additionally, the Commissioner gained the authority to seek injunctions, during an election period, to stop a contravention or force a person to comply with the act where fairness and the public interest warranted action. Formerly, the Commissioner was able to proceed only through the regular courts.

The legislation also standardized the process by which voters could register on the day of an election. Since 1993, both rural and urban voters had been permitted to register on election day, but only rural voters had the option to qualify, without documented evidence of identity and address, by simply making a sworn statement and having any other elector registered in that polling division vouch for them. Bill C-2 extended this option to urban voters as well.

The new *Canada Elections Act* clarified the rights of tenants and landlords with respect to campaign posters and signs. Under the new act, it is illegal for landlords to prohibit displays of election posters, although they may set reasonable conditions for the size or type of poster and may prohibit display of posters in common areas. Additionally, it is now an offence under the new act to deny candidates or their representatives access to an apartment building or condominium during an election period.

In modern election campaigns, advertising by political parties and candidates – using television, radio, newspapers, brochures, placards and other media – has become one of the ways in which voters receive information about the choices available to them. All advertising, including that of candidates and political parties, is prohibited on election day, with the exception of previously published advertising in pamphlets, on billboards or on signs. Another exception to this prohibition is Internet election advertising published before election day, if the advertisement did not change on election day. This restriction is intended to ensure that candidates have an opportunity to respond to any advertising made by their opponents before the polls open.

Court decisions have struck down the more extensive blackout period in previous legislation.

The Vote Through the Decades

1920 The *Dominion Elections Act* consolidates Parliament's control of the federal franchise, introduces advance voting and establishes the post of Chief Electoral Officer.

1921 The first federal election is held at which women vote on the basis of the universal franchise, which had been granted three years earlier, near the end of the First World War.

1930 The government of R. B. Bennett introduces a standing list of electors to replace enumeration, but abandons the approach as impractical and expensive after one election.

1950 Inuit are granted the right to vote.

1955 The last vestiges of religious discrimination are removed from the federal elections act.

1960 The government of John Diefenbaker extends the franchise unconditionally to "registered Indians."

1970 The voting age is lowered from 21 to 18; 18-year-olds vote for the first time in the 1972 general election.

1982 The *Canadian Charter of Rights and Freedoms* entrenches the right to vote and to be a candidate.

1992 Measures are formalized to ensure access to the vote for people with disabilities. The *Referendum Act* provides the legal and administrative framework for conducting federal referendums on any question related to the Constitution of Canada.

1993 The use of the special ballot is broadened to permit voting by anyone who cannot vote on election day or at an advance poll, including Canadians living or travelling abroad. Also, inmates serving sentences of less than two years, judges and people with mental disabilities are qualified for voting.

1996 The act is amended to provide for the establishment of the National Register of Electors, eliminating door-to-door enumeration.

1996 Longer and staggered voting hours are introduced.

2002 The Supreme Court decision in *Sauvé v. Canada* repeals the *Canada Elections Act* restriction of voting rights for inmates serving sentences longer than two years.

2004 All inmates can vote in the 2004 general election.

Many, many polling stations
More than 65,000 polling stations in every city, town and village across Canada were needed for the general election of January 23, 2006. Almost 15 million ballots were cast in that winter election, including more than 1.5 million during three days of advance voting.

The 2000 *Canada Elections Act* limits the blackout period only to the transmission of election advertising on polling day, until the close of all polling stations in the electoral district. The Supreme Court of Canada upheld this legislation in 2004.

Opinion polls have become an integral part of modern elections. Concerned that opinion polls published late in an election campaign could affect the outcome of the election, Parliament in 1993 adopted legislation banning publication of opinion polls during the 72 hours before election day. However, this provision was challenged in court as an infringement of freedom of speech, and, in its 1998 decision in *Thomson Newspapers Co. v. Canada (Attorney General)*, the Supreme Court of Canada struck it down as a violation of freedom of expression, ruling that the limits were unjustified under section 1 of the Charter.

At the same time, the court's ruling indicated that concerns about the methodological accuracy of polls were warranted, and that it would therefore be constitutional to invoke legislation requiring poll results to be accompanied by details about the methodology used. Consequently, the 2000 *Canada Elections Act* requires the initial publication of opinion polls to include details about the sponsor and the methodology of the survey. The new act also prevents the publication of the results of new or previously unpublished opinion polls on election day, for reasons similar to the ban of advertising on election day.

Boundary Redistribution

For the democratic process to be truly representative, a system for maintaining the fair and balanced distribution of constituency boundaries is essential. The Fathers of Confederation addressed this requirement in the *Constitution Act, 1867*, by adopting the basic working principle of "representation by population." Given that the act guaranteed Quebec a minimum of 65 seats in the House of Commons, the seat allotment for the rest of the country was determined by dividing the average population in Quebec's 65 ridings into the total population for each of the other provinces – thus making the number of seats per province proportional to their respective populations. The *Constitution Act, 1867* furthermore provided a mechanism for maintaining this balance by specifying that a process to review and adjust provincial seat allotments, as well as boundaries of individual ridings, should occur after each 10-year census.

Significantly, in those early years after Confederation, the responsibility for determining the

Readjusting Electoral Boundaries

The process of boundary readjustment, largely unchanged since the *Electoral Boundaries Readjustment Act* of 1964, works as follows:

1. **After each decennial census**, the Chief Statistician of Canada sends provincial population data to the Chief Electoral Officer, who applies the formula set out in the law to calculate how many seats are allotted to each province. (Since its first incarnation in the *Constitution Act*, this formula has changed many times in attempts to maintain fair representation in the face of shifting demographic realities.)
2. **Electoral boundaries commissions are established**, consisting of a chairperson – typically a provincial court judge – appointed by the chief justice of each province, and two residents of the province, appointed by the Speaker of the House of Commons. The commissions must begin deliberating on new electoral district boundaries within 60 days after the census data are sent.
3. **Each commission develops a redistribution plan** that is published in newspaper ads, along with times and locations for public hearings, at least 60 days before the first scheduled hearing. Upon written notice to the commission, any interested individual or group – including sitting MPs and senators – can speak at the hearings.
4. **Commissions must complete their reports**, typically, within a year of receiving the population data.
5. **A designated House of Commons electoral committee** receives the commissions' reports, by way of the Chief Electoral Officer and the Speaker of the House.
6. **MPs have 30 days to file written objections** to the reports, which must be signed by at least 10 MPs altogether. The committee then has another 30 days to discuss these objections, before returning the reports, with their comments, to the commissions.
7. **The commissions modify the reports** – or not, as they choose – then forward their final boundary decisions to the Chief Electoral Officer.
8. **The Chief Electoral Officer issues a draft representation order**, based on the commission reports, documenting names, populations and descriptions of the new electoral districts, and forwards this document to the responsible minister.
9. **Cabinet proclaims the representation order** within five days of its receipt, making the new boundaries public. Within five more days, Cabinet must publish the representation order and the proclamation declaring it to be in force in the *Canada Gazette*.
10. **At least one year must pass** between the date Cabinet proclaims the representation order and the date Parliament is dissolved for a general election before the new boundaries can be applied to that election.

new boundary placements rested solely with the government. The *Representation Act* of 1903 sought to rectify the consequent political advantage by conferring the job of boundary readjustment on a bipartisan committee of the House of Commons. Since the governing party still held a majority on the committee, though, the pursuit of balanced democratic representation remained a secondary consideration, and blatant political manoeuvring within the process continued to fuel rancorous debate for another 60 years.

In 1964, the *Electoral Boundaries Readjustment Act* (EBRA) established a genuinely impartial process for redrawing constituency borders in Canada – one that has remained essentially unchanged in the four decades since. The premise underlying the impartiality sought by EBRA is that the responsibility for boundary adjustment must be assigned

Shifting the Boundaries
The work of determining federal electoral district boundaries following each decennial census is done by 10 independent electoral boundaries commissions (one for each province). As Nunavut, the Northwest Territories and Yukon constitute one electoral district each, they do not require commissions or boundary changes. Pictured here is the commission for Ontario, at one of its 2002 hearings in London, during the most recent boundaries readjustment process.

to formally non-partisan bodies. To this end, the legislation provides for the appointment, in each province,* of an independent electoral boundaries commission to supervise the redistribution process.

While EBRA has proved itself significantly superior to its predecessors, no legislation can be expected to reign unchallenged over such a demographically sensitive function. With continual, volatile population shifts occurring since the 1970s, the EBRA process has led to new seats being created in southern, urban areas of the country at the expense of remote, northern and rural ridings, as well as some established and historic ridings in urban cores.

Ensuing Charter challenges have highlighted the concept of "community of interest" – the most significant case being *Carter v. Saskatchewan* (1991). The case was put forward on behalf of the Society for the Advancement of Voter Equality (SAVE), a group of Saskatoon and Regina voters seeking a court ruling on the constitutional validity of the electoral boundaries adopted by Saskatchewan after *The Representation Act, 1989* became law.** In reversing a decision by that province's court, the Supreme Court of Canada held that strict population count should not be deemed the only consideration in defining equitable electoral district boundaries. The court ruled that "the purpose of the right to vote enshrined in section 3 of the Charter is not equality of voting power per se, but the right to 'effective representation'," which could be achieved by "relative parity of voting power," taking factors such as geography, community history, community interest and minority representation into account, to "ensure that our legislative assemblies effectively represent the diversity of our social mosaic."

The most recent case highlighting the concept of community of interest was *Raîche v. Canada (Attorney General)* (2004), in which the Federal Court held that the Federal Electoral Boundaries Commission for New Brunswick had erred in its application of

*Territories are excepted, since each comprises a single riding – their boundaries, therefore, need no adjustment. This has been the case since 1999, when Nunavut was established and the two ridings making up the Northwest Territories were separated. (Yukon has held its single riding since becoming a distinct territory in 1898.)

**The act had resulted in the creation of seats in all but the northern part of the province with tolerance limits of plus or minus 25 percent. For the two northern seats, the limits were set at plus or minus 50 percent. It made a further distinction among the seats in the southern part of the province by dividing them into rural and urban categories. The 25 percent limit for southern seats represented a switch from Saskatchewan's previous population limits of plus or minus 15 percent, and the urban/rural distinction was a first in the province's history. (Courtney) the rules governing the preparation of its recommendations. The court found that the commission had not adequately heeded the importance of the *Official Languages Act* and the communities of interest that existed in the electoral districts. In response to this case, Bill C-36, which received royal assent in 2005, changed the boundaries of the Acadie–Bathurst and Miramichi electoral districts. This was the first time since the introduction of EBRA that a court had ordered that an electoral boundary be changed.

In 1994, the suspension of some sections of EBRA led to the drafting of Bill C-69: *An Act to provide for the establishment of electoral boundaries commissions and the readjustment of electoral boundaries.* Provisions in the proposed legislation were aimed largely at forging a closer link between the redistribution process and the real needs of the populations it sought to serve. It provided for redistribution reviews every five years, instead of 10, where warranted by significant population swings. It also defined the term "community of interest" to include

> … such factors as the economy, existing or traditional boundaries of electoral districts, the urban or rural characteristics of a territory, the boundaries of municipalities and Indian reserves, natural boundaries and access to means of communication and transportation.

Bill C-69 was passed by the House of Commons, but subsequently died on the Order Paper in the Senate when the 1997 general election was called.

Following the Representation Order of 2003, the Standing Committee on Procedure and House Affairs made a bid to address these problems in its April 2004 report to the House, offering several key recommendations for improving redistribution. The report drew on the extensive experience of the Subcommittee on Electoral Boundaries Readjustment, which the Committee had established to deal with objections of members of Parliament to the reports of the electoral boundaries commissions following the 2001 census. The Committee intended to highlight strengths and weaknesses in the redistribution process so that improvements could be found. Many of the recommendations sought to increase the transparency and accountability of the commissions by raising their public standing while maintaining their effectiveness and independence. The Committee made 21 recommendations, including one to appoint three federal judges to act as a national appeal tribunal. According to this recommendation, appeals could be put forward where significant opposition was registered, or where a commission did not make changes despite a mandatory second public review *and* a recommendation for change was made by a committee of the House of Commons. In a March 2005 response to one of the Standing

Populations in Canada move significantly over time. Who would have predicted the dramatic growth of the west at the time of Confederation? The political leaders at the time did not. This is obvious from the way they allocated seats to the Senate.

– Elwin Hermanson
Debate on Bill C-69
House of Commons, February 24, 1995

Table 4.1

Number of Provincial and Territorial Seats, 1867–2003

Year	Can.	N.B.	N.S.	Ont.	Que.	Man.	B.C.	P.E.I.	N.W.T.		Y.T.		N.L.	Nun.
1867	**181**	15	19	82	65									
1871	**185**	15	19	82	65	4								
1872	**200**	16	21	88	65	4	6							
1873	**206**	16	21	88	65	4	6	6						
1882	**211**	16	21	92	65	5	6	6						
1887	**215**	16	21	92	65	5	6	6	4					
1892	**213**	14	20	92	65	7	6	5	4					
1903	**214**	13	18	86	65	10	7	4	10		1			
									Alta.	**Sask.**	**N.W.T. /Y.T.**			
1907	**221**	13	18	86	65	10	7	4	7	10	1			
1914	**234**	11	16	82	65	15	13	3	12	16	1			
1915	**235**	11	16	82	65	15	13	4	12	16	1			
1924	**245**	11	14	82	65	17	14	4	16	21	1			
1933	**245**	10	12	82	65	17	16	4	17	21	1			
1947	**255**	10	13	83	73	16	18	4	17	20	1			
1949	**262**	10	13	83	73	16	18	4	17	20	1		7	
											N.W.T.	**Y.T.**		
1952	**265**	10	12	85	75	14	22	4	17	17	1	1	7	
1966	**264**	10	11	88	74	13	23	4	19	13	1	1	7	
1976	**282**	10	11	95	75	14	28	4	21	14	2	1	7	
1987	**295**	10	11	99	75	14	32	4	26	14	2	1	7	
1996	**301**	10	11	103	75	14	34	4	26	14	2	1	7	
2003	**308**	10	11	106	75	14	36	4	28	14	1	1	7	1

Committee's later reports, the government stated that it agreed with the need to improve the redistribution process and that this should occur before the next decennial census in 2011.

In May 2005, the Chief Electoral Officer issued a report entitled *Enhancing the Values of Redistribution*, which outlined his own recommendations following the Representation Order of 2003. The report was divided into five groups of recommendations, including:

- ways in which the timely conclusion of redistribution can be ensured
- amendments to enhance the effective representation of Canadians
- ways to improve the amount and quality of public input in the redistribution process, support mechanisms to assist commissions in completing their work and means to standardize the methods by which a commission's decisions can be reviewed
- a suggestion that the Federal Court of Appeal consider applications for review of commissions' decisions

The report also supported the calls from the Standing Committee to embed the term "communities of interest" in the legislation, by specifically proposing that

> … a commission shall recognize communities when doing so promotes or maintains the effective representation of members of the community. In applying the concept of community, the commission shall consider factors such as: demographic and sociological characteristics; boundaries of local government and administrative units; economic ties; and any other factor that the commission feels is demonstrative of the existence of a community.

Whatever EBRA's shortcomings are judged to be, there is little doubt that the legislation has generally served well over the five redistributions that have occurred since 1961 and has freed the process from gerrymandering. Despite the fact that the current system works well, refinements will undoubtedly be required to reflect the ongoing changes in regional populations and communities of interest while ensuring effective representation of Canadians.

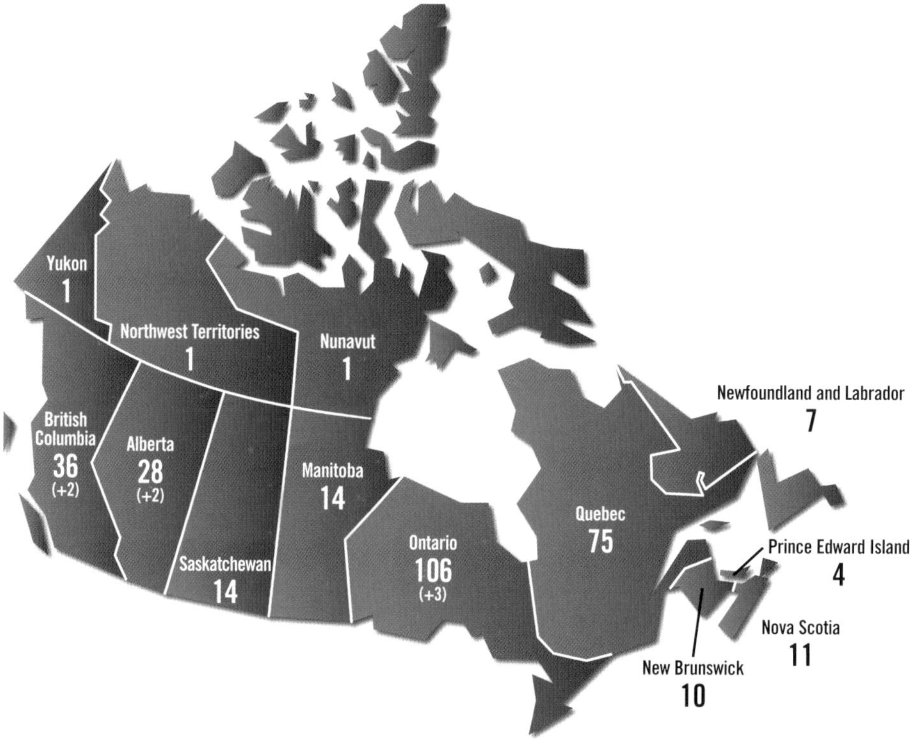

Electoral Districts per Province and Territory
The number of electoral districts (and seats in the House of Commons) rose by seven, to 308, when a new representation order came into effect with the dissolution of Parliament for the 2004 general election. As this map of districts per province and territory illustrates, the additional districts, reflecting changes in population, were allocated to British Columbia (2), Alberta (2) and Ontario (3).

Regulation of Political Parties, Candidates and Campaign Finance

From Confederation to the present, we have seen a steady expansion of the franchise as citizens' right to vote became the cornerstone of electoral law. For this right to be meaningful, however, citizens must be able, first, to choose among competing parties and candidates and, second, to support the validity of their choice by having access to information about the activities of the contestants. Yet the full disclosure of electoral activity required by today's standards is a strikingly recent innovation.

Concerns about the fairness of political competition and worries about donors exercising undue influence over politicians are hardly new themes in Canadian politics. In 1873, telegraph transcripts showed Sir John A. Macdonald demanding large campaign contributions from promoters of the Canadian Pacific Railway; the evidence helped topple his Conservative government – and prompted the succeeding Liberals to quickly adopt the *Dominion Elections Act*. In its first iteration, in 1874, the act required candidates and their "agents" (political parties were not recognized in law until nearly a century later) to disclose how and where campaign funds were spent. However, the act's provisions did not limit these expenses, require disclosure of contributions or even assign responsibility for administering and enforcing the legislation.

Further scandals continued to shake the House in the ensuing decades, countered by many new provisions in the act. In 1891, it became an offence to assist a candidate in exchange for money or other valuable consideration. In 1908, corporations were barred from making campaign contributions, while others could make donations only through a candidate's official agent. The lack of an overseeing body, however, made the legislation an ineffective deterrent, and businesses continued to donate campaign funds freely to whomever they wished.

Starting in 1920, candidates were required to reveal the names of contributors and the amounts of their donations. For nearly 50 years, these changes remained the last significant amendments to the election financing provisions of the act, despite the lingering deficiencies that would be exposed from time to time.

However, if the mid-twentieth century was marked by a prolonged inattention to the advancement of electoral financing provisions, the years from 1970 to the present redressed the lull with a flurry of legislation. It was during this period that political parties were first recognized in law – and the financial activities of political parties, candidates, third parties, nomination and leadership contestants, and local electoral district associations alike first became regulated. Also dating from this period is the position of Commissioner of Election Expenses, later designated the Commissioner of Canada Elections.

Recognition of Political Parties in Law

The Canadian constitution does not recognize the existence of political parties. Nevertheless, the freedoms of association and peaceful assembly are explicitly entrenched in the *Canadian Charter of Rights and Freedoms* (section 2) and may only be restricted on the basis of (as stated in section 1) "such reasonable limits prescribed by law as can be demonstrably justified in a free and democratic society."

Before 1970, the *Canada Elections Act* also did not recognize the existence of political parties. However, this situation was examined in 1966 by the Committee on Election Expenses (the Barbeau Committee), which contended that such legal recognition could be used to enable:

- equalization in the money available to electoral candidates
- access to information by requiring disclosure of electoral financing
- wider participation in politics by the electorate through a tax credit system

Barbeau considered these objectives fundamental to the development of the democratic system.

Following Barbeau's recommendations, the *Canada Elections Act* was amended in 1970 to include a process by which political parties could register and thereby receive legal recognition. This was an attractive innovation for party leaders because, by registering, a party was for the first time allowed to place its name on the ballot under that of its candidate in any electoral district. Given that candidate support is strongly influenced by party affiliation, this was an important piece of information to have on the ballot.

Registration became all the more significant a few years later, when, following recommendations from both Barbeau and the 1972 report from the Special House of Commons Committee on Elections Expenses (the Chappell Committee), Parliament adopted Bill C-203, the *Election Expenses Act*, in 1974. This was a significant new piece of legislation because, on the one hand, it required political parties to limit their election spending and report the sources of their contributions, but at the same time, it made them eligible to receive reimbursements for a portion of their election expenses.

Once political parties are recognized in law and become recipients of public funding, it is necessary to devise a means to determine what kind of entity qualifies for such benefits. The first approach to this came in the 1970 legislation, which stipulated that for a political party to qualify for registration and the associated benefits, it had to run candidates in at least 50 electoral districts.

Fifty Candidates Not Needed
Communist Party of Canada leader Miguel Figueroa went to court and successfully challenged a provision of the *Canada Elections Act* that required a political party to field 50 candidates in a general election to maintain its registration. Only registered parties that field at least one candidate have the right to list their party name on the ballot next to the candidate's name.

This requirement stood for many years before being challenged under the Charter by Miguel Figueroa, leader of the Communist Party of Canada. Founded in 1921 and registered under the *Canada Elections Act* since party registration began in 1974, the Communist Party was deregistered in 1993 because it failed to run 50 candidates in that year's general election. The Supreme Court of Canada's 2003 decision in *Figueroa v. Canada* struck down the 50-candidate requirement as an unjustifiable restriction on the rights guaranteed under the

Charter. The court determined there was no reason to believe that a political party running fewer than 50 candidates could not act as an effective outlet for the meaningful participation of individual candidates. The ruling also declared that restricting the ability of political parties to register was an unwarranted infringement on the right of citizens to play a meaningful role in the electoral process.

Thus in 2004, Parliament adopted Bill C-3*: *An Act to amend the Canada Elections Act and the Income Tax Act*, implementing new criteria for the registration of political parties. The intent of the bill, supported by both the government and the opposition parties, was to strike an appropriate balance between fairness to parties and the integrity of the electoral system.

Among the legislation's innovations was the country's first legal definition of a political party, which it described as

> … an organization one of whose fundamental purposes is to participate in public affairs by endorsing one or more of its members as candidates and supporting their election.

The bill also included new provisions for measuring political activity. Parties were required to maintain, at all times, the presence of a leader, three other officers and at least 250 members. Furthermore, parties had to submit an updated members list and signed declarations every third year and annually file a statement outlining the party's fundamental purpose. Failure to meet any of these conditions brought the risk of deregistration.

At committee stage in the House of Commons, a sunset provision was added to Bill C-3 to accommodate concerns with the new legislation. According to that provision, the amendments made by C-3 to the *Canada Elections Act* would retire two years after the legislation came into effect. On April 24, 2006, the government introduced Bill C-4, *An Act to amend An Act to amend the Canada Elections Act and the Income Tax Act*. Bill C-4 received royal assent on May 11, 2006. It replaces the sunset provision in Bill C-3 with a requirement for a mandatory review of the legislation, within two years, by a committee of the Senate and a committee of the House of Commons.

*Bill C-3 was the reinstated version of Bill C-51, which had not received royal assent when the previous session of Parliament was prorogued in November 2003 and so died on the Order Paper.

Reforming Electoral Finance

Before 1974, only the finances of candidates were regulated under electoral legislation, leaving all others free to promote the party or candidate of their choice to whatever extent they saw fit. In the opinion of the 1966 Committee on Election Expenses (Barbeau),

> … no group or bodies other than registered parties and nominated candidates [should] be permitted to purchase radio and television time, or to use paid advertising in newspapers, periodicals, or direct mailing, posters or billboards in support of, or opposition to, any party or candidate, from the date of the issuance of the election writ until the day after polling day.

Conceding that such limits might encroach somewhat on the freedom of third parties, the Barbeau Committee nonetheless concluded that without any restrictions, it would simply be impossible to limit and control election spending.

Barbeau's recommendation, however, extended only to expenditures aimed at directly opposing or endorsing parties or candidates during an election period. It did not support a ban of indirect expenditures (issue advocacy), believing that this would "stifle the actions of such groups in their day-to-day activities." In 1972, the Chappell Committee – while supporting Barbeau's position on direct expenditures – extended the recommendation to indirect expenditures as well.

In 1974, a Liberal minority government had a slim margin of seats over the opposition Progressive Conservatives, with the New Democratic Party holding the balance of power. It was a time when many closely related events caused concern about mushrooming election expenditures. To this were added all the ramifications of Watergate following the 1972 election in the United States. These events built up public concern about the impact of high election expenses on democracy, and they are said to have greatly influenced the adoption of the *Election Expenses Act* by Parliament in 1974. (Stanbury) This legislation established the first comprehensive set of financial rules for federal political parties.

A key innovation of the 1974 legislation was to impose limits on how much parties and candidates could spend during election campaigns. This measure was intended to prevent an upward spiral in spending and to make election contests fairer by ensuring that parties and candidates could not vastly outspend one another. This position has been upheld consistently since. For instance, the Lortie Commission, in its 1992 report, concluded that spending limits

> ... constitute a significant instrument for promoting fairness in the electoral process. They reduce the potential advantage of those with access to significant financial resources and thus help foster a reasonable balance in debate during elections. They also encourage access to the election process. (RCERPF, 336)

In 1993, a ban was imposed on political donations from foreign sources. (A decade after that, Bill C-24 and in 2006, Bill C-2 further restricted contributions and other aspects of electoral financing – see "Extending Public Funding and Regulation" on page 125.)

The 1974 legislation also made significant advances in spending transparency, which is a key consideration for any regulatory regime governing political finance. To make informed judgments about candidates and political parties, voters must have access to information about who is contributing to these parties and in what amounts. Embracing this principle, the *Election Expenses Act* required candidates and political parties to disclose the names and contribution amounts of all contributors donating more than $100. (This threshold was later raised to $200 under the 2000 *Canada Elections Act*.)

Also among the 1974 reforms were amendments to the *Broadcasting Act* (1968) that entitled registered political parties to an allotment of free and paid broadcasting time during elections. Radio and television stations were required to make available up to 6.5 hours of prime time for paid advertising or political broadcasts by registered parties during the last four weeks of the election campaign. Starting in 1983, this time was allocated among parties by the Broadcasting Arbitrator, who used a formula based on the party's popular vote and the number of seats it won in the previous election. As well,

Under the 1974 *Election Expenses Act*:

- Political parties and candidates were each given a limit on how much they could spend during election campaigns.
- Groups and individuals other than parties or candidates were prohibited from spending during elections to promote or oppose candidates, unless the expenditures were intended to gain support for a policy stance or to advocate the aims of a non-partisan organization.
- Both political parties and candidates were required to disclose the amount and the source of all contributions over $100.
- Registered political parties qualified for a partial reimbursement of their election expenses.
- Candidates who won at least 15 percent of the vote in their electoral districts were reimbursed a portion of their election expenses.
- Radio and television stations were required to make up to 6.5 hours of prime time available for paid advertising or political broadcasts by registered parties during the election campaign. This time was allocated among parties by the Broadcasting Arbitrator.
- Radio and television networks were required to make free-time programming periods available to registered parties.
- A maximum tax credit of $500 was available to individuals who contributed to political parties and candidates.

radio and television networks were required to make free-time programming available to registered parties during network-reserved time periods – although not necessarily in prime time. Broadcasters were not required to allot air time for individual candidates, but if they did, they would trigger an obligation to offer equal time for that riding's other candidates.

Another major innovation of the 1974 *Election Expenses Act* was to reimburse candidates and political parties for a portion of the money they spent campaigning in elections. Public funding in the form of reimbursements is intended to make political office more accessible to political parties and candidates that might not have wealthy financial backers. Under the system of reimbursements instituted in 1974, candidates were the major beneficiaries of public funding. Candidates who won at least 15 percent of the vote in their electoral districts became eligible for partial reimbursement of their election expenses. In 1974, the amount of the reimbursement was based on a formula taking into account the number of electors in the district. The legislation was changed in 1983 to make the reimbursement equal to 50 percent of the candidate's total election expenditures (and later 60 percent, under Bill C-24).

The 1974 act also instituted the reimbursement of certain election expenses for registered parties, compensating them for 50 percent of their total expenditures for television and radio advertising. In 1983, Bill C-169 defined a considerably broader scope and new eligibility rules for reimbursement, entitling parties to 22.5 percent of their *total* election expenses – but only if those expenses amounted to at least 10 percent of the allowable spending limit. In 1996, Bill C-243 adjusted the eligibility rules so that parties needed to have received at least 2 percent of the valid votes cast nationally or 5 percent of those cast in the electoral districts in which they ran candidates. Finally, in 2004, the reimbursement rate was increased from 22.5 percent of a party's paid election expenses to 60 percent for the first election after Bill C-24 came into force, dropping back to 50 percent for subsequent general elections.

The final important element of the 1974 reforms was to introduce the Political Contribution Tax Credit, which allows Canadians who make a contribution to a candidate or a registered political party to claim a generous credit on their income taxes. The tax credit is a way for government to finance political parties while rewarding those parties that successfully solicit donations from Canadians. The tax credit is the most generous for small contributions, so it encourages parties to solicit many small contributions from individuals, rather than a small number of large contributions from other sources. (In 2004, Bill C-24's enhancements to the credit – including doubling, to $400, the amount on which the maximum tax credit of 75 percent could be claimed – provided even further incentive for individual donors to support political parties. And in 2006, Bill C-2 took the next step by barring donations from corporations, trade unions and unincorporated associations altogether, leaving only individuals able to make political contributions.)

Third-Party Spending

In an effort to prevent circumvention of the spending limits for parties and candidates imposed by the 1974 *Election Expenses Act*, the legislation also established that only parties and candidates themselves would be permitted to spend money during an election period for the purpose of promoting or opposing candidates. In other words, expenditures

The Commissioner of Canada Elections

The 1974 *Election Expenses Act* also established the position of Commissioner of Election Expenses, which would oversee compliance with and enforcement of election expenses provisions in the *Canada Elections Act*. The position title was changed, in 1977, to Commissioner of Canada Elections, when these powers were extended to cover *all* provisions of the act. The Commissioner of Canada Elections:

- is appointed, and can be removed, by the Chief Electoral Officer
- functions independently of the government and political process
- since 1993, oversees a national network of investigators to carry out investigations in the field on his behalf
- up to 2006, had sole authority to prosecute for an offence under the *Canada Elections Act* (a unique power, since other federal acts assigned this responsibility to the Attorney General); now refers files to the Director of Public Prosecutions
- must investigate all complaints (which may be filed by any Canadian citizen) and decide whether to proceed
- is empowered by the 2000 *Canada Elections Act* to use injunctions and compliance agreements as enforcement tools
- is authorized to seek judicial deregistration of political parties that do not satisfy the new definition of a political party legislated under Bill C-3 (2004)

by so-called third parties – that is, any individual or group other than a candidate or a registered political party – were expressly prohibited, except where intended to gain support for a policy stance or promote the objectives of a non-partisan group. However, the act did offer a defence against prosecution under the new provisions if a defendant could show that such election expenses had been incurred "in good faith," or in other words, without any intent to act maliciously or take unfair advantage.

This wording proved so broad that it failed to stand up in court against most infractions, and it thereby undermined the intended effect of the spending restrictions. For this reason, the Liberal government, in 1983, introduced Bill C-169, which amended the legislation to prohibit *any* third-party election spending directed at supporting or opposing a candidate or party, unless officially authorized.

This legislation was struck down by the Alberta Court of Queen's Bench, in the case of the *National Citizens' Coalition Inc. v. Canada (Attorney General)* (1984), on the grounds that it was an unconstitutional infringement of freedom of expression under section 2 of the Charter. The government did not appeal, and the Chief Electoral Officer declared the decision applicable nationwide. This remained the status quo until 1993, when Bill C-114, based on recommendations of the Lortie Commission, sought to prohibit third parties from incurring election advertising expenses over $1,000. These restrictions, in turn, faced their own challenge from the National Citizens Coalition in *Somerville v. Canada (Attorney General)* (1996) – and met a similar fate, being struck down by the Alberta Court of Appeal. Again, the government did not appeal and the ruling stood.

A new legal interpretation of third-party spending restrictions emerged the following year, in *Libman and the Equality Party v. Attorney General of Quebec* (1997), a case involving provisions in that province's *Referendum Act* similar to those struck down federally in the *Somerville* case. In addressing the Alberta court's logic offered in *Somerville*, the Supreme Court of Canada found that limiting third-party spending as a means of promoting equality of participation was justifiable under the Charter, inasmuch as such regulations aim

> ... to permit an informed choice to be made by ensuring that some positions are

Canadian Public Opinion on Political Financing

Results from the Canadian Election Study (CES) conducted over the last decade show notable support for the regulation of political financing.

1997
- 83 percent of respondents support limitations on third-party expenditures

2000
- 94 percent of respondents agree that the public has the right to know how candidates and political parties obtain their contributions
- 93 percent support a cap on election expenses
- 63 percent support limits on campaign contributions

2004
- 72 percent of respondents agree that riding associations should be required to register with the Chief Electoral Officer
- 68 percent support the new limits on campaign expenses for nomination contestants
- 57 percent support banning corporations and unions from contributing directly to political parties

Source: www.ces-eec.umontreal.ca

> not buried by others [and] to preserve the confidence of the electorate in a democratic process that it knows will not be dominated by the power of money.

That same year, the *Report of the Chief Electoral Officer of Canada on the 36th General Election* urged legislators to correct the anomaly established by the *Somerville* ruling. This anomaly permitted third parties to spend an unlimited amount on election advertising, while the candidates themselves were restricted in their spending on election expenses. This circumstance, the Chief Electoral Officer declared, could "erode the financial foundation of the electoral system." He recommended that new legislation be drafted to restrict third-party spending, based on similar provisions in the federal *Referendum Act*.

The next attempt to restrict third-party spending activities materialized in September 2000 under Bill C-2 – the new *Canada Elections Act*. In this incarnation, election advertising was defined as

> … the transmission to the public by any means during an election period of an advertising message that promotes or opposes a registered party or the election of a candidate, including one that takes a position on an issue with which a registered party or candidate is associated.

The new provisions limited third parties, which are now defined in the *Canada Elections Act* as "a person or a group, other than a candidate, registered party or electoral district association of a registered party", to spending no more than $150,000 overall on election advertising and no more than $3,000 in a given electoral district (both amounts to be regularly adjusted for inflation). As proposed in the Chief Electoral Officer's 1997 report, the provisions also subjected third parties, for the first time, to registration and reporting requirements; these applied to any such entity that chose to spend more than $500 on electoral advertising during an election.

In 2000, the National Citizens Coalition challenged the legislation's constitutionality in *Harper v. Canada (Attorney General)*. As the timing of the case coincided with the running of that year's federal election, the Alberta Court of Queen's Bench issued an injunction preventing Elections Canada from enforcing the third-party spending provisions in Alberta while their constitutionality remained before the court. At that time, the Chief Electoral Officer applied the ruling nationwide, declaring it to be "in the public interest that the law be applied uniformly in a federal general election." However, he maintained, the other third-party provisions in the act – notably the registration and reporting requirements – would remain in force. Ultimately, though, even

All of us in this House have been guilty at one time or another of throwing out the accusation that corporate or union contributions influence our opponents – often without foundation. And the media even more so. This is not good for the political process. It is not good for democracy. This Bill addresses this issue head on.

– Jean Chrétien
Address preceding the second reading of Bill C-24
House of Commons, February 11, 2003

Changing the Political Financing Rules

In June 2003, Canada's Parliament made significant reforms to the political financing rules in the electoral legislation. Bill C-24 extended disclosure and registration requirements for political entities, introduced new limits on political contributions and imposed a ban on contributions from unions and corporations to political parties and leadership contestants. The amendments also introduced the payment of a quarterly allowance to registered political parties based on the percentage of votes each obtained in the previous general election.

these provisions were struck down when the Alberta Court of Appeal finally delivered its verdict in December 2002.

Further to an appeal by the government, the Supreme Court of Canada ruled on May 18, 2004, that, while the limits on third parties do violate freedom of expression, the impairment was minimal and therefore justified, given the capacity of these limits to promote equality, ensure voter confidence and protect the integrity of the overall regulation of political finance.

All provisions of the third-party legislation were therefore upheld.

Extending Public Funding and Regulation

By the end of the last century, a vigorous debate had arisen on the subject of campaign and electoral financing. Nomination and leadership campaign expenses were unregulated, and arguments raged over the continued influence of major corporate and union donors. Stringent laws governing political donations came into force in 1977 in Quebec and 2000 in Manitoba. In 1992, the Lortie Commission made several recommendations to reform political finace at the federal level.

In the Chief Electoral Officer's own reports to Parliament following the 1993, 1997 and 2000 general elections, Mr. Kingsley strongly supported measures to curb the influence of corporate and union donors. These reports proposed, in effect, that the control of money was a value that must be managed to some degree, setting "reasonable limits" that balanced the Charter right to liberty against the *Canada Elections Act*'s fundamental need to establish equality and transparency.

In June 2002, in a bid to instill higher ethical accountability in government and to enhance the fairness and transparency of the electoral process, the government announced a comprehensive set of new ethics guidelines for Cabinet. These guidelines would, among other things, govern ministerial activities for personal political purposes, transform the financing of political parties and candidates, and generally strengthen public service management and accountability for public funds. Introducing the second reading of Bill C-24, the Right Honourable Jean Chrétien said that this bill was designed to

> ... address the perception that money talks. That big companies and big unions have too much influence on politics. A Bill that will reduce cynicism about politics and politicians.
>
> Debates *February 11, 2003*

In June 2003, Parliament adopted Bill C-24: *An Act to amend the Canada Elections Act and the Income Tax Act* (see box, next page), which provided the most significant set of reforms to party and campaign finance since the 1974 *Election Expenses Act*.

The legislation was rooted in the belief that the primary source for contributions to political parties and candidates should be individuals giving relatively small amounts, as opposed to larger donations. The new regulations, therefore, stipulated that each elector could contribute up to a total of $5,000 a year to the electoral district associations, nomination contestants and candidates of a registered political party, while donations to these entities from corporations and trade unions were limited to $1,000. Furthermore, while individuals could contribute directly to the registered party, corporations and unions could not. To police the new rules, the act also stipulated that candidates and parties should disclose contribution information within a set period of time after an election, and leadership contestants should do so during and after a leadership contest.

As a counterbalance to the new contribution limits, however, Bill C-24 also introduced significant ongoing public financing for political parties. These provisions entitled any party receiving a minimum percentage of the popular vote in a general election to an annual public allowance proportional to its share of votes. The concept was not new – both the Barbeau Committee in 1966 and the Lortie Commission in 1992 acknowledged that funding for political parties through direct public subsidies was a good idea. Bill C-24 introduced annual allowances, recognizing that parties should be compensated for the loss of their customary funding stream from large

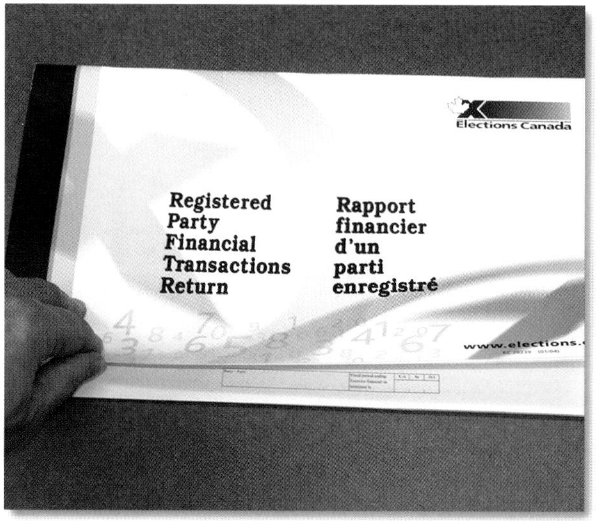

Disclosure Rules Extended to Other Political Entities

To ensure that the rules for contribution and spending limits are followed, all candidates and registered political parties are required by law to report their financial activities to the Chief Electoral Officer. In 2003, amendments to the *Canada Elections Act* and the *Income Tax Act* extended disclosure requirements to include other political entities, such as registered electoral district associations and nomination and party leadership contestants.

corporate and union donations – and that the political party is arguably the focal point of a vibrant and viable democratic system.

Bill C-24 also sought to address concerns about unbridled spending in nomination and leadership contests. New rules required candidates in these contests to:

- register with Elections Canada
- abide by rules governing who could make contributions to their campaigns
- limit nomination campaign expenses to 20 percent of the general election spending limit for that electoral district, per candidate
- disclose all nomination contributions and spending information as they would for election campaigns

Finally, following recommendations from the Lortie Commission, the Hawkes Committee and the Chief Electoral Officer, Bill C-24 brought constituency associations of registered parties (known as local electoral district associations) under legislative

Key Provisions of Bill C-24 (2004)

- Individual Canadian citizens and permanent residents could contribute up to $5,000 annually to a registered party and its electoral district associations, candidates and nomination contestants, plus an additional $5,000 toward a party leadership contest and $5,000 to each independent candidate.
- Corporations and trade unions could contribute up to $1,000 annually to a registered party's electoral district associations, candidates and nomination contestants – but nothing at all to the party itself or its leadership contestants.
- Anyone who accepts a contribution to his or her campaign for the leadership of a party, or incurs leadership campaign expenses, must apply to the Chief Electoral Officer to register as a leadership contestant.
- Registered political parties receive an annual allowance of $1.75 for each vote they won in the most recent general election. To qualify, a party needs to have received at least 2 percent of all votes cast nationally or 5 percent of votes cast in the electoral districts in which it ran candidates.
- The election expenses reimbursement rate for registered parties increased from 22.5 to 50 percent.
- The share of votes cast that a candidate must receive to qualify for election expenses reimbursement was lowered from 15 to 10 percent, while the portion of eligible expenses increased from 50 to 60 percent.
- The upper threshold for a donation eligible to receive the maximum Political Contribution Tax Credit rate of 75 percent rose from $200 to $400.
- New anti-avoidance provisions prohibited attempts by parties or candidates to hide the identity of donors or otherwise circumvent restrictions on contributor eligibility or contribution amounts.
- The period for instituting a prosecution following the commission of an offence was extended from 18 months to seven years, as long as the action commenced within 18 months of the complaint being brought to the attention of the Commissioner of Canada Elections.

control for the first time. Under the new rules, any such entity wishing to accept contributions on behalf of – or provide goods and services, or transfer funds to – a registered party or candidate had to register and report annually to Elections Canada.

The underlying premise of Bill C-24 was that financial controls and full disclosure "will increase public confidence in the system, and that financially healthy political parties will contribute to the vitality of the electoral process." (Robertson, 13)

Bill C-24 was followed in 2006 by Bill C-2, known as the *Federal Accountability Act*. This legislation further restricted political donations and made other changes to the *Canada Elections Act* intended to increase the transparency of the electoral process and better control the influence of money on elections.

Key Provisions of Bill C-2 (2006)

- Only citizens and permanent residents of Canada may make donations to registered political entities.
- Donations are capped at $1,000 (indexed for inflation) per calendar year to each of the following:
  - any registered political party
  - the various entities of each registered party (registered associations, nomination contestants and candidates)
  - each independent candidate for a particular election
  - the contestants in a particular leadership contest
- Cash contributions to registered political entities are limited to $20.
- Corporations, trade unions, associations and groups may no longer make political contributions.
- Candidates cannot accept any gift (other than contributions to their campaign) that might be seen to influence them as eventual members of Parliament, although they may accept a gift from a relative or as a normal expression of courtesy or protocol.
- Candidates must report to the Chief Electoral Officer the name and address of every person (other than a relative) or organization from whom they receive a gift or gifts worth more than $500 while a candidate, the nature of the gift and the circumstances under which it was given.
- Registered parties and registered electoral district associations may no longer transfer trust funds to candidates of the party.
- The Chief Electoral Officer is responsible for appointing a returning officer for each electoral district. Appointments are made on the basis of merit, when the Chief Electoral Officer is satisfied that the person meets the essential qualifications to perform the work. Returning officers are appointed for a term of 10 years, but may be removed for reasons set out in the act.
- A prosecution for an offence under the *Canada Elections Act* must start within five years after the day when the Commissioner became aware of the facts giving rise to the prosecution, and no later than 10 years after the day the offence was committed.
- The Director of Public Prosecutions is responsible for initiating and conducting prosecutions for offences under the *Canada Elections Act*. The Commissioner of Canada Elections remains responsible for compliance agreements and enforcing the act through the use of injunctions to prevent or stop violations of the law during an election period.

It's All on the Web

In keeping with Elections Canada's mandate to inform Canadians about the electoral process, an extensive Web site at www.elections.ca publishes past election results and provides explanations of how to register and vote, electoral legislation, a searchable database on political financing and a search tool allowing electors to obtain information about electoral districts.

Mapping the Electoral Districts

Elections Canada and Natural Resources Canada publish maps showing the new electoral boundaries resulting from every redistribution process. The name, description, population and map of each electoral district in Canada are assembled into atlases for each province and territory. This set of atlases shows the federal electoral districts as set out in the most recent Representation Order, proclaimed on August 25, 2003 (for the provinces), or in the *Constitution Act, 1867* (for the territories).

Technology and the Electoral Process

During the last decade, new technologies have drastically changed the way elections are administered in Canada, becoming not merely a source of efficiency but, in many respects, part of the process itself.

Canada's first significant step toward high-tech election administration began in 1992, with a computerized list of electors. This innovation made possible the development of the National Register of Electors, which was established in 1997 after Bill C-63 came into force. By the 2000 general election, the cost of establishing the Register had already been recouped, and by 2004, the administrative savings had pushed the initiative some $30 to $40 million ahead of its business case at the federal level alone. Following the 2006 general election, savings attributable to the Register were estimated to be some $110 million. (For further information, please see the earlier section, The National Register of Electors.)

Computer technology has also greatly improved the administration of election financing, particularly the registration of political entities and disclosure of their contributions and expenses. Returns are posted on the Elections Canada Web site as they are submitted, verified, then re-posted, giving the public timely access to all election financing data. The Web site also enables quick and easy dissemination of updates to forms and information when new financing provisions are added to the *Canada Elections Act*.

As well, digital cartography is being applied to display election information on computerized maps, to further assist returning officers, candidates and political parties during elections. The geographic databases also provide the framework for locating electors inside an electoral district and assigning them to a polling division ("geocoding") and readjusting electoral boundaries after a decennial census. They also allow electors to enter a postal code on Elections Canada's Web site to obtain information on the corresponding electoral district, member of Parliament and polling station.

By October 2005, 91 percent of elector addresses were "georeferenced" (that is, linked to a point on a computerized map). For the 2006 general election, geographic documents that included 69,752 original maps were produced. Political parties received computer-readable versions of all of these maps, as well as access to the related Web application, GeoExplore.

Elections and referendums are now managed through a networked computer application called the Event Management System (EMS), which links each electoral district returning office to Elections Canada in Ottawa. This system allows electronic monitoring of election activities against deadlines and statutory obligations. With daily information sharing, EMS helps measure the effectiveness of election delivery systems by providing a consolidated picture of organizational activities. It also helps returning officers to monitor election material inventories and progress on election tasks within their own electoral districts.

On election night, meanwhile, Canadians are served by a Web module called Election Night Results (ENR). Once the polls are closed across the country, ENR posts election results as they unfold, with a 30-second refresh rate that conveys them virtually the instant a polling station reports its updates of the vote counts.

Elections Canada's Web site presents extensive information on the Canadian electoral process, including historical data and past election results. The Web site also includes publications that can be read or ordered on-line, a searchable database on electoral financing, recent research on and policy analyses of Canada's electoral system, current legislation, and the status of reforms and redistribution processes. Political parties and candidates can also find extensive information on electoral legislation, as well as on-line forms to assist them in filing necessary reports. The site's popularity burgeoned between 1998 and 2006 from some 6,000 monthly visitors to over 300,000. Visits to the Web site during the 2006 general election reached 3,347,270 – more than double the 1,580,672 visits during the 2004 general election.

Technologies have also been implemented to assist persons with disabilities, including teletypewriter (TTY) service for people with hearing impairment, campaign news releases on audio news and other information services for persons with visual impairment, and a voice response system on the inquiries line that directs people to where they should vote.

Finding an Electoral District
GeoExplore is a computer application that helps users locate federal electoral districts, polling divisions and sites, and civic addresses anywhere in Canada. It generates maps on-line to serve returning officers, field liaison officers, members of Parliament, political parties, provincial electoral agencies and Elections Canada staff.

Election Night Results

On each election night, after all of the polls are closed, the Elections Canada Web site provides preliminary voting results for each electoral district. They are also displayed nationally, by province or territory, by major centre and by party leader. During the following few days, the site also shows the official results as validated by each returning officer and the results of judicial recounts in districts with close totals for the two candidates receiving the most support.

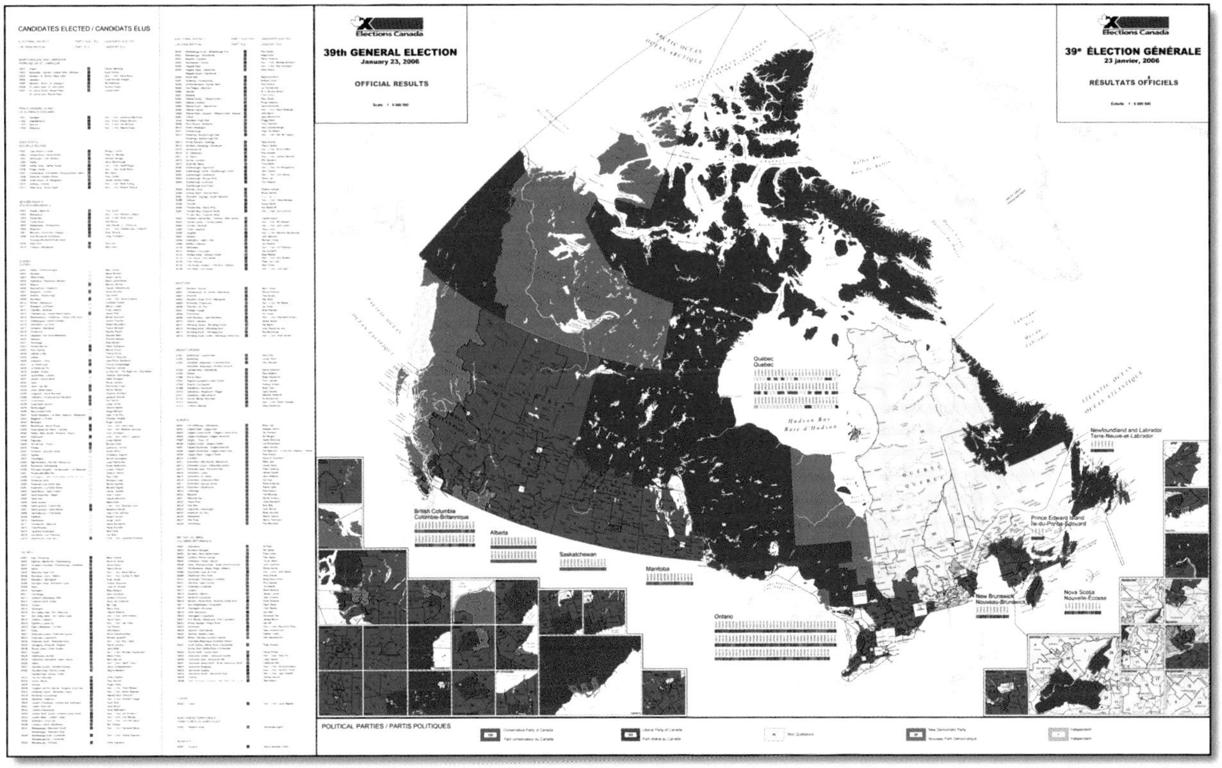

Participating in Democratic Development Abroad

The 1989 collapse of the Berlin Wall signalled a new chapter in the history of democratic development, and the past decade has seen the rapid emergence of new democracies all over the world. Canada has made significant contributions to the process of democratization by fostering international co-operation in a number of fields. The electoral process is central to this new wave of international democratic co-operation.

Democracy is the only form of government that recognizes and protects the intrinsic value and equality of each individual, thereby holding human rights at its very core. It has been demonstrated that democratic government brings other benefits as well – including increased economic development. Among the basic institutions required for democracy to be truly effective are well-enforced legal protections for human rights, a functioning opposition and a free press to hold the government accountable as well as an auditor general (or the functional equivalent) to ensure that citizens know how public resources are being allocated and spent. But the primary goal of democratic development must be the creation and support of institutions and processes that uphold the values of freedom, equality and justice – among them, a valid electoral process.

In this context, the role of non-partisan electoral management bodies is central to the conduct of free and fair elections. International electoral participation involves much more than observation at election time. Election monitoring can also be considered an opportunity to promote democratic principles and practices and to share expertise and ideas.

Recognizing that democratic development projects can benefit greatly when electoral management bodies work together in networks of support, Elections Canada has contributed to international democratic development by entering partnerships and fostering co-operation with other agencies and organizations working in this area – at both the national and international levels, and by collaboration with various national and international organizations.

Since 1980, Elections Canada has coordinated Canada's participation in hundreds of events in some 100 countries, primarily technical and professional support missions and observation or monitoring missions, and has received numerous foreign delegates visiting Canada who wish to learn more about the Canadian electoral system.

The agency offers support and accompaniment based on respect for the sovereignty, culture and history of the country in which electoral events are taking place, as well as for the independence of local electoral management bodies. The purpose of such participation is to build mutually beneficial relationships through the exchange of information and expertise, whereby all those involved learn from the experience.

If we begin with the premise that democracy is always a work in progress – even in countries like Canada – then we can better understand why democratic development is such a complex area of activity. Like democracy itself, democratic development is always perfectible.

– Jean-Pierre Kingsley
Institute for Research on Public Policy Conference
Keynote speech, September 10, 2004

These principles have been demonstrated by the evolving nature of the agency's international electoral partnerships. International assistance and co-operation ranges in effort from a small, one-time sharing of information to long-term, multi-faceted partnerships with other electoral management bodies. An example of the latter is the long-standing relationship with Mexico's Federal Electoral Institute, which began in 1993 and included the signing of two five-year bilateral co-operation agreements (in 1996 and 2001).

More recent examples of the application of these principles are the International Mission for Iraqi Elections, established in December 2004, and the International Mission for Monitoring Haitian Elections, established in June 2005, both chaired by the Chief Electoral Officer. The approach taken by these missions is one of accompaniment – that is, the establishment of close ties with the electoral commissions involved, over and above traditional electoral observation, with peer review and the sharing of analyses and information on an ongoing basis. This approach, though unique to the world of international electoral observation, is in reality

The International Mission for Iraqi Elections

Since 1990, Elections Canada has participated in about 400 international democratic development missions, assisting some 100 different countries. One important project was the December 2004 establishment of the International Mission for Iraqi Elections (IMIE), supported by the United Nations, the Independent Electoral Commission of Iraq and the government of Canada. Under the chairmanship of Canada's Chief Electoral Officer, the IMIE monitored election preparations and voting in Iraq, and it serves as an ongoing model for international collaboration in election monitoring.

a continuation of the kind of relationship Elections Canada has developed and fostered for a number of years on a bilateral basis.

While the work of supporting democratic consolidation in various countries remains far from complete, the ongoing nature of this work reflects a fundamental principle of social change – that democracy is never fully achieved. It is always a work in progress. This truth applies to long-standing democracies, such as Canada, as much as to those that are newly emerging.

Conclusion

The Charter era, which began in 1982, has been characterized by a bevy of electoral reforms stemming from two distinct sources: the courts, responding to dozens of Charter-based challenges; and the executive and legislative branches, following recommendations by various parliamentary committees, a royal commission – and, notably, the reports of the Chief Electoral Officer.

Indeed, the markedly more substantive content of these reports is a reflection of the obligation to address the escalating influence of the *Canadian Charter of Rights and Freedoms*. By granting individual Canadians legal recourse to challenge federal legislation, the Charter has triggered electoral reform at an unprecedented pace. Meeting the demands of this new era has made legislators aware of the value of the unique experience afforded the country's head election administrator. If the need for input from this office became increasingly evident over the Charter's first decade, it has since become firmly established.

The changes in electoral legislation arising in the Charter era, particularly through the 1990s and into this century, have resulted in greater access to the vote and better administrative practices to ensure that the electoral system has the flexibility to meet the evolving needs of the electorate. With advance polls, the special ballot, polling day registration and uniform level access at polling places, virtually all Canadians age 18 or older have both the right to vote and the means to do so. Interestingly, despite the many improvements in access to the vote in recent years, approximately 87 percent of the electors who exercised their franchise in the 2006 general election chose to do so at an ordinary polling station on election day.

At the same time, regulation of election finances and activities of political parties, candidates and third-party supporters has lent further substance to voting rights; by controlling the influence of money on elections in this country, these provisions have greatly advanced fairness and transparency in elections and the values held by Canadians generally.

Despite many advances to ensure that Canadians' access to the franchise is both universal and meaningful, a sizable portion of the electorate still does not exercise its right to vote. This presents a significant challenge for electoral administration. Although voter turnout increased between the 2004 and 2006 general elections, the need to continue attracting electors to the democratic process remains. In response, Elections Canada has focused attention on citizens whose electoral turnout tends to be low, especially young Canadians, Aboriginal people, ethnocultural minorities and special needs communities. Research findings suggest that the priorities of these groups may differ from those of other voters and may therefore cause them to interact with the political process in a different manner.

Nothing in democracy is set in stone. The evolution of legislation reflects that fact, as do the ever-changing values of citizens. At the time of writing this book, the *Federal Accountability Act* had just received royal assent, affecting political financing, the appointment of returning officers and the way in which investigation and prosecution of those who break electoral laws are carried out. Other legislation still before Parliament that could set fixed federal election dates, modify the length of senatorial terms of office and establish a process of consultation with electors about appointments to the Senate, would also transform democracy in Canada.

As we have seen throughout this book, the rights and institutional protections that are the legacy of history are not static or impervious to change. But the very qualities that make them flexible and adaptable to shifting social values also make them fragile and potentially vulnerable. Like democracy itself, they are living entities that must be tended with care and given the means to flourish. This is the challenge that must be met afresh by each new generation of voters.

APPENDIX

Voter Turnout Since Confederation

The history of the vote in Canada is the history of an almost constantly expanding right, despite temporary detours along the way. By the time of the 1921 general election, Canada had achieved almost universal suffrage.

EXPANSION OF THE franchise is evident in the figures on electoral participation – often referred to as voter turnout. The number of registered electors rose from 361,028 at Confederation to over 23 million in 2006 (see Table 1). In 1867, the electorate represented just 11 percent of the population; by 2006, this proportion had grown to over 75 percent.

Although expansion of the electorate is partly the result of population growth, the electorate also grew significantly following changes in electoral laws to broaden the franchise. For example, the enfranchised proportion of the population increased from 25 percent in 1911 to more than 50 percent in 1921, following the enfranchisement of women and the removal of property requirements for voters. Increases in electoral participation have also resulted from legislative and administrative changes intended to simplify registration and voting procedures, thereby facilitating exercise of the franchise.

In the 39 general elections and three referendums held since 1867, an average of 71 percent of registered electors exercised the franchise. Voter turnout, which is calculated based on the number of individuals registered to vote, has ranged from a low of 44 percent in the Prohibition plebiscite of 1898 to a high of 79 percent at the general election of 1958.

Significant variations in voter turnout are shown in Table 2. Turnout rates have generally been higher in Prince Edward Island, Nova Scotia and New Brunswick than in the other provinces. With the exception of the 1958 general election, average voter turnout in Newfoundland and Labrador has consistently been below that of other provinces.

Studies of voting behaviour in the past two decades, often supported by extensive public opinion polling, have suggested several factors that help to explain variations in turnout. Regional variations, for example, have been explained in terms of electoral competitiveness, with higher rates of turnout being associated with a higher proportion of competitive electoral contests. Studies have also shown that socio-economic status tends to influence voter participation: electoral participation increases with levels of education and income. In addition, members of some occupational groups have been found to participate at lower rates than other groups in society.

Characteristics such as race and ethnicity, language and religious affiliation have been found to affect electoral behaviour, but the rate of voter turnout among women and men has tended not to differ significantly. Age also affects turnout. Until recently, the finding that turnout is lower among youth than among older people was believed to be largely the result of a "life cycle" effect: young people's propensity to vote was found to increase as they aged. Recent studies indicate that this explanation no longer holds. Not only are young people participating less than their elders, their willingness to participate appears to be declining over time.

Following the June 2004 election, Elections Canada began a unique study to determine actual voter turnout among different age groups by analyzing samples of voters lists. The findings showed that first-time voters (those between 18 and 21½ years of age) had a 39 percent voter turnout. This made them about 4 percent more likely to vote than those eligible to vote for their second time (those between 21½ and 24 years of age).

Elections Canada is conducting a similar study after the 39th general election to find out if any clear trends emerge.

The relative stability or mobility of the population has been identified as a determinant of voter turnout. Electoral districts with a disproportionately mobile population tend to have lower rates of turnout. Other predictors of political participation include political interest, political knowledge and strength of party identification. The most interested and informed individuals are more likely to vote or participate in the political process in other ways. Because interest in politics can influence turnout, the issues in a given election campaign can be important indicators of potential participation.

Finally, the electoral process itself can influence voter turnout. Qualifications determining eligibility, the registration process, the available methods of voting, and information about electoral rights and procedures – all can have an effect on turnout. Illness and hospitalization or absence from home for other reasons are often cited as reasons for not voting, as are weather conditions at various times of the year. Electoral officials cannot change the weather, but some obstacles to voting can be tackled through administrative and practical means. In fact, some changes in the law originated as practical innovations in election administration.

Table 1

Voter Turnout at Federal Elections and Referendums, 1867–2006*

Date of election/referendum	Population	Number of electors on lists	Total ballots cast	Voter turnout[1] (%)
August 7 – September 20, 1867[2]	3,230,000	361,028	268,387	73.1
July 20 – October 12, 1872	3,689,000	426,974	318,329	70.3
January 22, 1874	3,689,000	432,410	324,006	69.6
September 17, 1878	3,689,000	715,279	534,029	69.1
June 20, 1882	4,325,000	663,873	508,496	70.3
February 22, 1887	4,325,000	948,222	724,517	70.1
March 5, 1891	4,833,000	1,113,140	778,495	64.4
June 23, 1896	4,833,000	1,358,328	912,992	62.9
September 29, 1898[3]	4,833,000	1,236,419	551,405	44.6
November 7, 1900	4,833,000	1,167,402	958,497	77.4
November 3, 1904	5,371,000	1,385,440	1,036,878	71.6
October 26, 1908	5,371,000	1,463,591	1,180,820	70.3
September 21, 1911	7,204,527	1,820,742	1,314,953	70.2
December 17, 1917	7,591,971	2,093,799	1,892,741	75.0
December 6, 1921	8,760,211	4,435,310	3,139,306	67.7
October 29, 1925	8,776,352	4,608,636	3,168,412	66.4
September 14, 1926	8,887,952	4,665,381	3,273,062	67.7
July 28, 1930	8,887,952	5,153,971	3,922,481	73.5
October 14, 1935	10,367,063	5,918,207	4,452,675	74.2
March 26, 1940	10,429,169	6,588,888	4,672,531	69.9
April 27, 1942[3]	11,494,627	6,502,234	4,638,847	71.3
June 11, 1945	11,494,627	6,952,445	5,305,193	75.3
June 27, 1949	11,823,649	7,893,629	5,903,572	73.8
August 10, 1953	14,003,704	8,401,691	5,701,963	67.5
June 10, 1957	16,073,970	8,902,125	6,680,690	74.1
March 31, 1958	16,073,970	9,131,200	7,357,139	79.4

*Presenting these figures involves several challenges. The data contained in official election results since Confederation have not been reported consistently. In the case of an election by acclamation, for instance, the number of registered electors on the lists for that electoral district was included in the total number of registered electors for some elections, but not for others. In other cases, lists of electors were not prepared for some districts. In Prince Edward Island, no lists were prepared in the entire province for several elections.

Moreover, a number of electoral districts were dual-member constituencies until 1966. As each elector could vote for more than one candidate, the reported number of votes cast (valid and rejected ballots) was higher than it would have been in a single-member scenario. Voter turnout figures (including those presented in this Appendix) have been corrected where appropriate: to estimate turnout in these cases, the total number of votes cast in a plural-member electoral district was divided by the number of members elected from that district. (Scarrow 1962)

Table 1

Voter Turnout at Federal Elections and Referendums, 1867–2006 (continued)

Date of election/referendum	Population	Number of electors on lists	Total ballots cast	Voter turnout[1] (%)
June 18, 1962	18,238,247	9,700,325	7,772,656	79.0
April 8, 1963	18,238,247	9,910,757	7,958,636	79.2
November 8, 1965	18,238,247	10,274,904	7,796,728	74.8
June 25, 1968	20,014,880	10,860,888	8,217,916	75.7
October 30, 1972	21,568,311	13,000,778	9,974,661	76.7
July 8, 1974	21,568,311	13,620,353	9,671,002	71.0
May 22, 1979	22,992,604	15,233,653	11,541,000	75.7
February 18, 1980	22,992,604	15,890,416	11,015,514	69.3
September 4, 1984	24,343,181	16,774,941	12,638,424	75.3
November 21, 1988	25,309,331	17,639,001	13,281,191	75.3
October 26, 1992[3, 4]	20,400,896	13,725,966	9,855,978	71.8
October 25, 1993	27,296,859	19,906,796	13,863,135	69.6[5]
June 2, 1997	27,296,859	19,663,478	13,174,698	67.0
November 27, 2000	28,846,761	21,243,473	12,997,185	64.1[6]
June 28, 2004	30,007,094	22,466,621	13,683,570	60.9
January 23, 2006	30,007,094	23,054,615	14,908,703	64.7

1. Percentages are calculated based on the number of registered electors.
2. In early elections, polling took place over several weeks or even months.
3. A referendum.
4. Does not include Quebec, as Quebec conducted its own referendum.
5. This percentage rises to 70.9 when the number of electors on the lists is adjusted to account for electors who had moved or died between the enumeration for the 1992 referendum and the election of 1993. A separate enumeration for the 1993 election was carried out only in Quebec, as the 1992 electoral lists were reused in all other provinces and territories.
6. Originally published as 61.2 percent, the 2000 turnout was adjusted to 64.1 percent, after normal maintenance of the National Register of Electors that removed the names of deceased electors and duplicates arising from moves.

Source: Reports of the Clerk of the Crown in Chancery (1867–1917); reports of the Chief Electoral Officer (1921–2006); unpublished summary data prepared by Elections Canada; R. Pomfret, *The Economic Development of Canada* (1987); H. A. Scarrow, *Canada Votes* (1962); *Contact* (1985).

Table 2

Voter Turnout[1] at Federal Elections and Referendums by Province and Territory[2]

Date of election/referendum	N.L.	P.E.I.	N.S.	N.B.	Que.	Ont.	Man.	Sask.	Alta.	B.C.	N.W.T.	Yukon	Nunavut	Canada
August 7 – September 20, 1867			77	71	69	75								73
July 20 – October 12, 1872			59	80	67	72	86			51				70
January 22, 1874		••	67	66	62	71	70			58				70
September 17, 1878		65	79	73	67	68	51			70				69
June 20, 1882		••	71	73	67	70	32			68				70
February 22, 1887		86	81	77	68	69	46			56	70			70
March 5, 1891		77	75	69	66	63	42			47	64			64
June 23, 1896		74	68	70	66	61	50			40	71			63
September 29, 1898[3]		46	40	41	46	47	32			30	38			45
November 7, 1900		••	77	73	70	70	65			69	76			77
November 3, 1904		••	73	77	70	77	69			56	72			72
October 26, 1908		••	73	78	69	68	81	••	••	54		87		70
September 21, 1911		••	83	78	71	69	79	63	65	53		83		70
December 17, 1917		76	80	89	76	79	79	70	76	83		56		75
December 6, 1921		79	69	64	75	63	65	67	63	67		83		68
October 29, 1925		76	70	61	72	65	68	57	57	75		78		66
September 14, 1926		84	72	68	71	64	77	70	57	71		80		68
July 28, 1930		89	83	78	76	69	72	81	66	73		82		73
October 14, 1935		80	76	77	74	74	75	77	65	76		70		74
March 26, 1940		78	70	68	66	69	74	77	63	76		82		70
April 27, 1942[3]		57	45	63	76	64	67	59	65	69	62	58		71
June 11, 1945		81	72	78	73	75	76	85	73	80		63		75
June 27, 1949	58	85	75	79	74	75	72	79	69	69		76		74
August 10, 1953	57	83	72	78	69	67	59	74	63	65	63	76		67
June 10, 1957	52	85	81	81	72	74	74	81	73	74	63	89		74
March 31, 1958	79	88	84	85	79	79	80	82	74	76	74	90		79

Table 2

Voter Turnout[1] at Federal Elections and Referendums by Province and Territory[2] (continued)

Date of election/referendum	N.L.	P.E.I.	N.S.	N.B.	Que.	Ont.	Man.	Sask.	Alta.	B.C.	N.W.T.	Yukon	Nunavut	Canada
June 18, 1962	72	90	84	83	78	80	77	85	74	78	72	88		79
April 8, 1963	69	84	82	81	76	81	78	83	79	80	73	88		79
November 8, 1965	66	88	82	80	71	77	74	80	74	75	76	86		75
June 25, 1968	68	88	82	80	72	77	76	81	73	76	69	87		76
October 30, 1972	63	86	80	77	76	79	74	79	76	73	73	79		77
July 8, 1974	57	80	74	71	67	74	70	72	67	72	61	67		71
May 22, 1979	60	81	75	74	76	78	77	79	68	75	70	74		76
February 18, 1980	59	79	72	71	68	72	69	71	61	71	67	69		69
September 4, 1984	65	85	75	77	76	76	73	78	69	78	68	78		75
November 21, 1988	67	85	75	76	75	75	75	78	75	79	71	78		75
October 26, 1992[3]	53	71	68	72	[4]	72	71	69	73	77	70	70		72
October 25, 1993	55	73	64	69	77	67	68	69	65	67	63	70		70[5]
June 2, 1997	55	73	69	73	73	66	63	65	59	66	59	70		67
November 27, 2000	57	73	63	68	64	58	62	62	60	63	52	64	54	61
June 28, 2004	49	71	62	63	61	62	57	59	59	63	47	62	44	61
January 23, 2006	57	73	64	69	64	67	62	65	62	64	56	66	54	65

• • Data not available

1. Percentages are calculated based on the number of registered electors.
2. The provinces entered Confederation as follows: New Brunswick, Nova Scotia, Ontario and Quebec, July 1, 1867; Manitoba, July 15, 1870; British Columbia, July 20, 1871; Prince Edward Island, July 1, 1873; Alberta and Saskatchewan, September 1, 1905; and Newfoundland, March 31, 1949.
3. A referendum.
4. Quebec conducted its own referendum in 1992.
5. See Table 1, note 5.

Source: Reports of the Clerk of the Crown in Chancery (1867–1917); reports of the Chief Electoral Officer (1921–2006); unpublished summary data prepared by Elections Canada.

Selected Readings

Abella, Irving Martin. "The 'Sydenham Election' of 1841." *Canadian Historical Review* Vol. 47, No. 4 (December 1966).

Abbott, Elizabeth, ed., and Jacques Legrand. *Chronicle of Canada*. Montréal: Chronicle Publications, 1990.

Adachi, Ken. *The Enemy That Never Was: A History of the Japanese Canadians*. Toronto: McClelland and Stewart, 1976.

Bacchi, Carol. "Liberation Deferred: The Ideas of the English-Canadian Suffragists, 1877–1918." Ph.D. thesis. McGill University, 1976.

Black, Jerome H. "Reforming the Context of the Voting Process in Canada: Lessons from Other Democracies." *Voter Turnout in Canada*, ed. Herman Bakvis. Vol. 15 of the research studies of the Royal Commission on Electoral Reform and Party Financing. Toronto and Oxford: Dundurn Press, 1991.

Brodie, Janine, with the assistance of Celia Chandler. "Women and the Electoral Process in Canada." *Women in Canadian Politics: Toward Equity in Representation*, ed. Kathy Megyery. Vol. 6 of the research studies of the Royal Commission on Electoral Reform and Party Financing. Toronto and Oxford: Dundurn Press, 1991.

Canada. Royal Commission on Electoral Reform and Party Financing (RCERPF). *Reforming Electoral Democracy*. Volumes 1 and 2 of the Final Report. Ottawa: RCERPF, 1991.

The Canadian Gallup Poll Ltd. "Attitudes of the Public Towards the Federal Electoral Process in Canada." Commissioned by Elections Canada. 1979.

———. "Attitudes of the Public Towards the Federal Electoral Process in Canada." Commissioned by Elections Canada. 1980.

———. "Gallup National Omnibus Conducted for Elections Canada: Summary of Results." Commissioned by Elections Canada. 1984.

———. "Gallup National Omnibus Conducted for Elections Canada: Summary of Results." Commissioned by Elections Canada. 1986.

Cleverdon, Catherine L. *The Woman Suffrage Movement in Canada*. Toronto: University of Toronto Press, 1950.

Cornell, Paul G., et al. *Canada, Unity in Diversity*. Toronto: Holt, Rinehart and Winston, 1967.

Courtney, John C. *Commissioned Ridings: Designing Canada's Electoral Districts*. Montréal and Kingston: McGill-Queen's University Press, 2001.

Dictionary of Canadian Biography (DCB). Volumes IV (1979), V (1983), VII (1988), VIII (1985), X (1972). Toronto: University of Toronto Press, 1966–.

Diefenbaker, John G. *One Canada: Memoirs of the Right Honourable John G. Diefenbaker. The Crusading Years 1895–1956*. Vol. 1. Toronto: Macmillan of Canada, 1975.

Eagles, Munroe. "Voting and Non-voting in Canadian Federal Elections: An Ecological Analysis." *Voter Turnout in Canada*, ed. Herman Bakvis. Vol. 15 of the research studies of the Royal Commission on Electoral Reform and Party Financing. Toronto and Oxford: Dundurn Press, 1991.

English, John. *The Decline of Politics: The Conservatives and the Party System 1901–20*. Toronto and Buffalo: University of Toronto Press, 1977.

Fenton, William N. *The Great Law and the Longhouse: A Political History of the Iroquois Confederacy*. Norman, Okla.: University of Oklahoma Press, 1998.

Franquet, Louis. *Voyages et mémoires sur le Canada*. With a preface by Jacques Lacoursière. Montréal: Éditions Élysée, 1974.

Gallup Canada Inc. "Gallup National Omnibus Survey of Eligible Voters." Commissioned by Elections Canada. 1988.

———. "1992 Federal Referendum Study: Volume I – National Survey Final Report." Commissioned by Elections Canada. 1993.

Garner, John. *The Franchise and Politics in British North America, 1755–1867.* Toronto: University of Toronto Press, 1969.

Hamel, J. M. "Canadian Women and the Vote." *Chelsea Journal* (September/October 1975).

Hamelin, Jean, and Marcel Hamelin. *Les mœurs électorales dans le Québec de 1791 à nos jours*. Montréal: Éditions du Jour, 1962.

Hamelin, Jean, John Huot and Marcel Hamelin. *Aperçu de la politique canadienne au XIXe siècle*. Québec: Presses de l'Université Laval, 1965.

Lamoureux, Diane. *Citoyennes? Femmes, droit de vote et démocratie*. Montréal: Éditions du remue-ménage, 1989.

Lavergne, France. *Le suffrage féminin*. Études électorales. Sainte-Foy: Directeur général des élections du Québec, 1990.

Milen, Robert A. "Aboriginal Constitutional and Electoral Reform." *Aboriginal Peoples and Electoral Reform in Canada*, ed. Robert A. Milen. Vol. 9 of the research studies of the Royal Commission on Electoral Reform and Party Financing. Toronto and Oxford: Dundurn Press, 1991.

Mishler, William. *Political Participation in Canada: Prospects for Democratic Citizenship*. Toronto: Macmillan, 1979.

Pammett, Jon H. "Voting Turnout in Canada." *Voter Turnout in Canada*, ed. Herman Bakvis. Vol. 15 of the research studies of the Royal Commission on Electoral Reform and Party Financing. Toronto and Oxford: Dundurn Press, 1991.

Pammett, Jon H., and Lawrence LeDuc. *Explaining the Turnout Decline in Canadian Federal Elections: A New Survey of Non-voters*. Ottawa: Elections Canada, 2003.

Pomfret, Richard. *The Economic Development of Canada*. Scarborough: Nelson Canada, 1987. Original published by Methuen Publications, 1981.

Power, Charles Gavan. *A Party Politician: The Memoirs of Chubby Power*. Edited by Norman Ward. Toronto: Macmillan of Canada, 1966.

Preston, W. T. R. *My Generation of Politics and Politicians.* Toronto: D.A. Rose Publishing Co., 1927.

Qualter, T. H. *The Election Process in Canada*. Toronto: McGraw-Hill Company of Canada, 1970.

Robertson, James R. *Bill C-24: An Act to amend the Canada Elections Act and the Income Tax Act (political financing)*. Legislative Summary. Parliamentary Research Branch, Library of Parliament, 2003.

Roy, Patricia E. "Citizens Without Votes: East Asians in British Columbia, 1872–1947." *Ethnicity, Power and Politics in Canada*, eds. Jorgen Dalhie and Tessa Fernando. Toronto: Methuen, 1981.

Ryerson, Stanley Bréhaut. *Unequal Union: Confederation and the Roots of Crisis in the Canadas, 1815–1873.* Toronto: Progress Books, 1973. Originally published in 1968.

Scarrow, Howard A. *Canada Votes: A Handbook of Federal and Provincial Election Data.* New Orleans: The Hauser Press, 1962.

———. "Patterns of Voter Turnout in Canada." *Voting in Canada*, ed. John C. Courtney. Scarborough: Prentice-Hall, 1967.

Schull, Joseph. *Laurier: The First Canadian*. Toronto: The Macmillan Co. of Canada, 1965.

Small, David, ed. *Drawing the Map: Equality and Efficacy of the Vote in Canadian Electoral Boundary Reform.* Vol. 11 of the research studies of the Royal Commission on Electoral Reform and Party Financing. Toronto and Oxford: Dundurn Press, 1991.

Stanbury, W. T. *Money in Politics: Financing Federal Parties and Candidates in Canada.* Vol. 1 of the research studies of the Royal Commission on Electoral Reform and Party Financing. Toronto and Oxford: Dundurn Press, 1991.

Stewart, Gordon T. "John A. Macdonald's Greatest Triumph." *Canadian Historical Review* Vol. 63 (1982), pp. 3–34.

Ward, Norman. *The Canadian House of Commons: Representation.* Toronto: University of Toronto Press, 1963.

Woodsworth, J. S. *Strangers Within Our Gates, or, Coming Canadians.* Toronto: F. C. Stephenson, 1909.

Index

Credits

Every effort has been made to trace copyright ownership and assign appropriate credit. We regret any inadvertent errors or omissions.

Abbreviations

LAC	Library and Archives Canada
RG	Record Group
MG	Manuscript Group
CIN	*Canadian Illustrated News*
CMCP	Canadian Museum of Contemporary Photography
DAP	Documentary and Art Photography

Cover
Detail of a sculpture entitled *The Vote*, carved in Indiana limestone on the east wall of the House of Commons chamber. © Eleanor Milne, Chris Fairbrother and Marcel Joanisse

Introduction
page xii
LAC, MG 55/24, no. 9, horizontal cabinet drawer 64, file 7, negative no. C-60168.

page xiii
LAC, DAP, CIN, vol. VI, September 7, 1872, p. 149, negative no. C-58780.

page xiv
G. Lunney, CMCP, N.F.B. Collection, no. 63-2051.

Chapter 1
Opening page
"The Montreal Elections – Meeting of the Victorious Candidates, East and West, at Viger Square" (artist unknown, Montréal, 1872), LAC, CIN, vol. VI, September 7, 1872, p. 152, negative no. C-58781.

page 2
LAC, DAP, negative no. C-13951.

page 3
LAC, DAP, 1988-93 (Lane of Books Collection), negative no. PA-165422.

page 4
LAC, negatives no. C-18408 and C-18409 (filing notation).

page 6
Nova Scotia Archives and Records Management, RG E, volume 1, no. 8.

page 7
Left, LAC, RG 4, B72 (Clerk of the Crown in Chancery Records), volume 40, p. 8131, horizontal cabinet drawer 64, file 5, negative no. C-135534. *Right*, LAC, DAP, 1970-62 (Roch Rolland Collection), item 16, negative no. PA-165451. *Bottom*, LAC, RG 14, C1 (Parliament, Legislative Council – Sessional Records), vol. 129, n. p., negative no. C-135540.

page 8
LAC, MG 23, G III 22 (Moses Hart Papers), negative no. C-7963.

page 10
"Partie orientale de la Nouvelle-France ou du Canada," map, 1755, Musée McCord Museum, Montréal.

page 11
LAC, DAP, 1973-72 (George A. MacInnis Collection), negative no. C-18,097.

page 17
Robert Auchmaty Sproule (1799–1845), *View of the Harbour, Montreal*, 1830, Musée McCord Museum, the David Ross McCord Collection, M303.

page 20
Robert Auchmaty Sproule (1799–1845), *St. James Street, Montreal*, 1830, Musée McCord Museum, the David Ross McCord Collection, M300.

page 23
LAC, DAP, CIN, volume 1, January 3, 1863, p. 91, negative no. C-124199.

page 24
Queen's University Archives, Collection 2139 (Morris Papers), box 3.

page 27
Left, LAC, DAP, 1933-261 (Samuel McLaughlin Collection), negative no. C-10671. *Right*, LAC, DAP, 1965-82 (Nedo Paveskovic Collection), negative no. C-36094.

page 28
Metropolitan Toronto Reference Library, Baldwin Room, broadside collection.

page 30
LAC, DAP, 1984-81 (J.-J. Girouard Collection), item 48, negative no. C-18,441 (transcript).

page 34
LAC, DAP, negative no. C-13947.

page 37
LAC, DAP, 1952-43 (Adèle de Guerry Languedoc Collection), negative no. C-51,818.

Chapter 2
Opening page
"Nomination Day Crowd" (photographer unknown, Renfrew, Ontario, February 15, 1912), LAC, DAP, 1974-286 (Harry Hinchley Collection), negative no. PA-94788. The occasion was made necessary by the resignation of Thomas Andrew Low (1871–1931) just two months after the 1911 general election.

page 40
LAC, CIN, volume XVIII, September 28, 1878, p. 193, negative no. C-68,249.

page 41
LAC, DAP, 1977-181 (S. Rettie Collection), negative no. PA-110153.

page 42
Top, LAC, MG 30, E 471 (Henri LaMothe Papers), volumes 1 and 4, files 1-36 and 4-3. *Bottom*, LAC, MG 26a (Sir John A. Macdonald Papers), volume 335b, p. 152,163, negative no. C-135611.

page 43
LAC, CIN, volume VI, August 31, 1872, p. 140, negative no. C-58,774.

page 44
LAC, DAP (Merrilees Collection), negative no. C-120987.

page 45
LAC, DAP, CIN, volume iv, July 1, 1871, p. 4, negative no. C-56,351.

page 49
LAC, negative no. C-78604.

page 51
LAC, MG 26A (Sir John A. Macdonald Papers), volume 69, p. 27588, negative no. C-6536.

page 52
LAC, MG 26A (Sir John A. Macdonald Papers), volume 69, p. 27583, negative no. C-6533.

page 53
LAC, MG 28, IV 3 (Liberal Party Records), negative no. C-122035.

page 54
LAC, DAP, CIN, May 4, 1878, p. 228, negative no. C-67,823.

page 55
LAC, negative no. C-97640.

page 57
LAC, DAP, 1971-120 (John Boyd Collection), item 2862, negative no. PA-60819.

pages 58, 59
LAC, DAP, 1964-114 (Department of National Defence, World War I Collection), negative nos. PA-2318 and PA-554.

page 61
LAC, DAP, 1966-094 (Cyril Jessop), negative no. PA-030212.

page 62
LAC, RG 4, B72 (Lower Canada and Canada East: Clerk of the Crown in Chancery, Election Records), volume 21, pp. 3153–54.

page 65
British Columbia Archives, negative no. HP-39849.

page 67
LAC, DAP, 1964-114 (Department of National Defence, World War I Collection), negative no. PA-2279.

Chapter 3
Opening page
Election preparations (circa 1957), Elections Canada.

page 70
Pierre Gaudard, N.F.B. Collection, CMCP.

page 71
Left, LAC, William James Topley Collection, series C, item 141159, negative no. PA-027012. *Right*, LAC, negative no. C-135522.

page 72
Elections Canada.

page 73
LAC, Elections Canada collection, negative no. C-135536.

page 74
Canadian Press photo, Archives of Manitoba (CPT11-8-2)jwp.

page 75
Pierre Gaudard, N.F.B. Collection, CMCP, no. 63-3289.

page 76
LAC, C-29452, copyright Milne Studios Ltd., Toronto.

page 77
Len Norris, *The Vancouver Sun*, used by permission.

page 78
LAC, George Sutekichi Miyagawa collection, item 1, negative no. PA-103542.

page 80
LAC, Arthur Roy Collection. *Left*, negative no. PA-047609. *Right*, negative no. PA-047135.

page 81
Pierre Gaudard, N.F.B. Collection, CMCP.

page 82
LAC, negative no. C-22001.

pages 84, 85
Elections Canada.

page 86
LAC, negative no. PA-190699.

page 87
J. Marshall, N.F.B. Collection, CMCP.

pages 88, 89, 90, 91
Elections Canada.

page 92
LAC, DAP, 1971-271, N.F.B. Collection, item 66020, negative no. PA-169812.

Chapter 4
Opening page
Polling stations (2004), Elections Canada.

pages 95, 97, 98
Elections Canada.

page 100
Top left, *Montreal Daily News*. *Others*, Elections Canada.

page 102
Elections Canada.

page 103
Cpl. John Bradley, 3 R22eR Bn Gp.

pages 107, 109, 111
Elections Canada.

page 113
Will Fripp, Secretary, Federal Electoral Boundaries Commission for Ontario.

page 118
Canadian Press (Kevin Frayer).

pages 125, 126, 129
Elections Canada.

page 133
Canadian Press/Abaca Press (Paul Assaker).